EXPLORING

FRENCH

Second Edition

Joan G. Sheeran
J. Patrick McCarthy

Consultant
Sarah Vaillancourt

EMC Publishing, Saint Paul, Minnesota

with special thanks to:

David and Leslie Neira—musical editing, general
and photographic assistance
James Douglas Sheeran—editorial advice
Judy G. Myrth—reading, editing, suggestions and
other assistance
Mary Jo Horan—artistic inspiration
Jackie Urbanovic—illustrations
The Nancekivell Group—cover design
*Paul Renslo, Eileen Slater and the students of Oak-
Land Junior High School*—photographic
assistance
Christine M. Gray—desktop production
Christine Gensmer—project management

photo credits:

Mike Woodside Photography—cover
NASA—Earth
Rick Armstrong—p. xii (t)
Janet Berry—p. vii (br)
A.G. Fralin and Christiane Szeps-Fralin—p. vi (b),
p. vii (t), p. viii (b), p. ix (bl, br), p. x (tl, bl),
p. xi (bl, br)
Ned Skubic—p. iii (all), p. vi (t), p. viii (t), p. ix (t),
p. x (r), p. xi (t)
Swiss National Tourist Office—p. vii (bl)
Sarah Vaillancourt—p. xii (bl, br)

ISBN 0-8219-1193-7

Published by EMC/Paradigm Publishing
875 Montreal Way
St. Paul, Minnesota 55102

Printed in the United States of America
4 5 6 7 8 9 10 XXX 99 98

INTRODUCTION

Bonjour et bienvenue!

Hello and welcome! You are about to explore a world where over 200 million people communicate in French every day. You will learn some common words and expressions that these people use daily. If you learn these basic words and expressions and if you have the opportunity to travel to one of the countries where people speak French, you will be able to understand some of the things they say. Also they will be able to understand you. As the world continues to shrink and as countries and people grow closer and closer together, it is important to be able to communicate with each other.

If you practice correct pronunciation with your teacher or with the audiocassettes, you will learn to speak French even better. Besides being able to understand and speak basic French, you will find out some information about France and get some insight into the country's rich traditions in art, music and literature. Hopefully, throughout your journey

you will discover that learning French is fun and not too difficult. Be sure to practice your French at every opportunity both in and outside of class. As with any other skill, the more you practice, the better you will become.

So, let's get started! *Allons-y!*

Table of Contents

1 GREETINGS AND EXPRESSIONS OF COURTESY
Salutations et Courtoisies 1

2 CLASSROOM OBJECTS
Les Objets de la salle de classe 8

3 CLASSROOM COMMANDS
Les Ordres donnés en classe 16

4 NUMBERS
Les Nombres 20

5 GEOGRAPHY
La Géographie 27

6 HOUSE
La Maison 38

7 FAMILY
La Famille 45

8 OCCUPATIONS
Les Professions et les Métiers 51

9 FOOD
La Nourriture 56

10 ART
L'Art 63

11 PARTS OF THE BODY
Les Parties du corps 70

12 CLOTHING
Les Vêtements 79

13 TIME AND COLORS
L'Heure et les Couleurs 86

14 MUSIC
La Musique 92

15 WEATHER AND SEASONS
Le Temps et les Saisons 97

16 DAYS AND MONTHS
Les Jours et les Mois 105

17 LITERATURE
La Littérature 114

18 LEISURE AND RECREATION
Les Loisirs et les Divertissements 120

19 SHOPPING
Les Achats 128

20 TRAVEL AND TRANSPORTATION
Les Voyages et les Moyens de transport 136

Exploring

...countries and cities

Quebec, Canada

Bonifacio, Corsica

Paris, France

Dakar, Senegal

Lucerne, Switzerland

Quebec, Canada

France

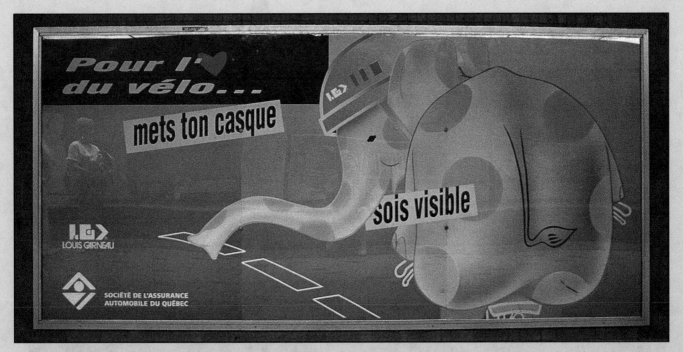

Montreal, Canada

Paris, France

Paris, France

Martinique

Montreal, Canada

Paris, France

Quebec, Canada

Arcachon, France

France

...and culture.

Paris, France

Paris, France

Chenonceaux, France

GREETINGS AND EXPRESSIONS OF COURTESY
Salutations et Courtoisies

Bonjour.
Good day. Hello. Good morning.
Bonsoir.
Good evening.
Bonne nuit.
Good night.

Courtoisies.

S'il te plaît. —— Please.
Merci. —— Thank you.
De rien. —— You're welcome.
Pardon. —— Excuse me.
Je regrette. —— I'm sorry.

Salut. —— Hi.
Au revoir. —— Good-bye.
À bientôt. —— See you later.
À demain. —— See you tomorrow.

Oui. Non.

Bonne chance.

GOOD LUCK.

Comment t'appelles-tu?
What's your name?

Je m'appelle Luc.
My name is Luc.

Tu parles français, n'est-ce pas?
You speak French, don't you?

Oui. Je parle français.
Yes. I speak French.

Comment vas-tu?
How are you?
Comment ça va?

Bien, merci. Et toi?
Fine, thanks. And you?

Pas mal. Ça va.
Not bad. All right.

Enchanté.
Pleased to meet you.

Parles-tu français?
Do you speak French?

Non. Je ne parle pas français.
No. I don't speak French.

Avec plaisir. — Pleased to meet you. (With pleasure.)
allemand (German), espagnol (Spanish), anglais (English), italien (Italian), russe (Russian)

À tout seigneur, tout honneur.   Treat all people courteously.

Je m'appelle...

Annette	Antoine
Antoinette	Bernard
Blanche	Bertrand
Brigitte	Charles
Claire	Didier
Constance	Étienne
Danielle	François
Denise	Guy
Florence	Henri
Françoise	Hervé
Isabelle	Jacques
Janine	Jean-Marcel
Jeanne	Louis
Lorraine	Michel
Marcelle	Patrice
Marie	Paul
Michelle	Pierre
Monique	René
Véronique	Robert
Yvette	Yves

Exercises

A Choisis l'expression inapplicable. *Choose the word that does not fit.*

1. Oui.	Enchanté.	Avec plaisir.	Bonjour.
2. À demain.	Au revoir.	Pardon.	À bientôt.
3. Bonne nuit.	Bonne chance.	Bonjour.	Bonsoir.
4. S'il te plaît.	Merci.	Bonjour.	De rien.
5. allemand	anglais	espagnol	Non.

B Choisis les noms de filles. *Choose girls' names.*

1. Danielle	6. Florence
2. Olivier	7. Patrice
3. Yves	8. Jean-Marcel
4. Jeanne	9. Monique
5. Pierre	10. Marie

C Réponds en français aux questions. Écris tes réponses. *Answer the questions in French. Write your answers.*

1. Comment t'appelles-tu? _____

2. Comment ça va? _____

3. Parles-tu français? _____

D Écris en français une expression pour chaque illustration. *Write in French an expression that corresponds to each picture.*

1. _____

2. _____

> Comment ça va?
> Salut!
> Je m'appelle...
> Merci.
> S'il te plaît.

3. _____

4. _____

5. _____

6. _____

7. _____

E Short answers. (En français, s'il te plaît.)

1. How do you say "hello"?

   _____.

2. An expression used to wish someone luck is

   _____.

3. How do you greet someone in the evening?

   _____.

4. *Non* is the opposite of

   _____.

5. An expression at an introduction is

   _____.

6. *Salut* is used to greet: a) M. Dubois   b) Monique

   _____   _____.

7. Answer this question: « Comment t'appelles-tu? »

   _____.

8. Complete this sentence:

   « _____ français. »

9. A colloquial version for *bonjour* is

   _____.

10. *Please* means

   _____.

F Réponds aux questions. *Answer the questions.* (En français, s'il te plaît.)

1. Denise: Bonjour, Didier. Comment vas-tu?

   Didier: _____

2. Florence: Salut! Je m'appelle Florence. Et toi?

   Bernard: _____

3. Olivier: Parles-tu français?

   Janine: _____

Mots croisés

G

Vertical

1. Good evening.
2. I speak.
3. « Avec...! »
4. « De... »
5. « À...(*later*)! »
6. Pleased to meet you.
8. « ...t'appelles-tu? »
10. Fine.
14. Yes.
15. All right.

Horizontal

1. Good day!
3. Excuse me!
7. « ...plaisir! »
9. Opposite of *oui*.
11. Thank you.
12. Night.
13. And you?
16. French.
17. Good-bye.

me voilà!

Nous avons la joie de vous annoncer la naissance de *Marie-Alix*

SALUT MICKEY!

EURO DISNEY

LES CARTES COULEURS DU MONDE

☐ RESTAURANTS ☐ HEBERGEMENT

Découvrez les prénoms de l'année

LISTE DES PRENOMS

LE CARNET DU JOUR

Pour recevoir le livret des prénoms envoyez une enveloppe timbrée à 5,00 F avec vos nom et adresse :
LE FIGARO
Le Carnet du Jour - Les prénoms de l'année
25, avenue Matignon 75008 Paris

BIENVENUE,

BON APPETIT,

BONNE NUIT.

BONNE ANNÉE

Bonjour la France !

CLASSROOM OBJECTS

Les Objets de la salle de classe

2

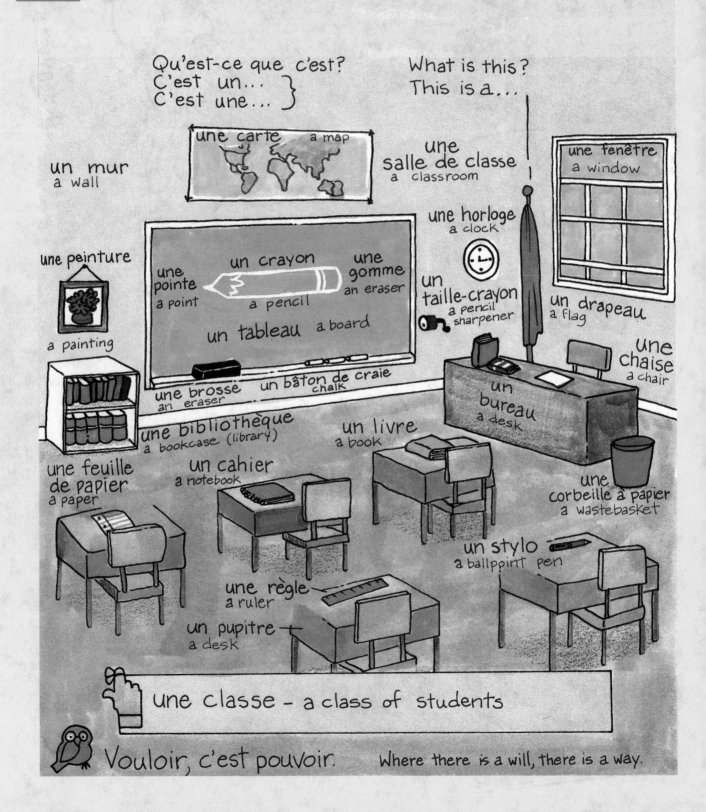

Qu'est-ce que c'est?
C'est un...
C'est une... }

What is this?
This is a...

une carte — a map

un mur
a wall

une
salle de classe
a classroom

une fenêtre
a window

une peinture

une horloge
a clock

un crayon

une
pointe
a point

une
gomme
an eraser

un
taille-crayon
a pencil
sharpener

un drapeau
a flag

a pencil

un tableau   a board

a painting

une
chaise
a chair

une brosse
an eraser

un bâton de craie
chalk

un
bureau
a desk

une bibliothèque
a bookcase (library)

un livre
a book

une feuille
de papier
a paper

un cahier
a notebook

une
corbeille à papier
a wastebasket

un stylo
a ballpoint pen

une règle
a ruler

un pupitre
a desk

une classe - a class of students

Vouloir, c'est pouvoir.   Where there is a will, there is a way.

Exercises

A Listening Comprehension

Your teacher will point out twenty-four classroom objects. As your teacher pronounces each object in French, find it on the list below and place the appropriate number after it.

un stylo _____   une feuille de papier _____

une règle _____   une horloge _____

une pointe _____   une bibliothèque _____

un cahier _____   un pupitre _____

une corbeille à papier _____   un taille-crayon _____

une peinture _____   un mur _____

un crayon _____   une fenêtre _____

une gomme _____   un bureau _____

un livre _____   une carte _____

une brosse _____   un tableau _____

un drapeau _____   une chaise _____

une classe _____   un bâton de craie _____

B Answer each question in English.

1. What are the colors of the "drapeau"? _____.

2. What does one put on a "mur" in order to decorate a room? _____.

3. What does the "horloge" indicate? _____.

C Choisis la réponse correcte. *Choose the correct response.*

1. Ink is used in a . . . .
   a) "un bâton de craie"   b) "stylo"

2. In the classroom the "bureau" belongs to the . . . .
   a) teacher   b) student

3. The "salle de classe" is . . . .
   a) small   b) large

4. One sits on a . . . .
   a) "cahier"   b) "chaise"

5. An eraser is found . . . .
   a) at the end of a "crayon"   b) on top of the "drapeau"

D   Écris en français le nom de chaque objet. *Write the French name for each object.*

1. _____

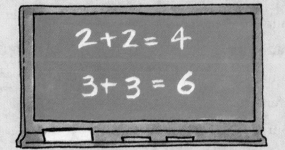

2. _____

3. _____

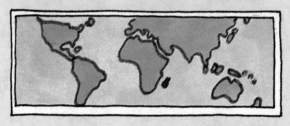

4. _____

5. _____

6. _____

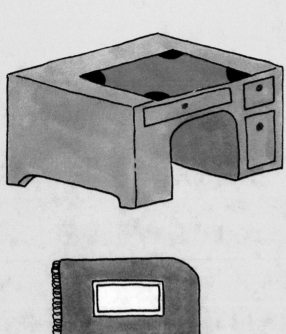

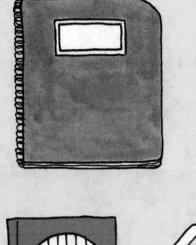

7. _____

8. _____

9. _____

10. _____

Dust Free

11. _____

12. _____

13. _____

14. _____

15. _____

E   Complète les phrases. *Complete the sentences.*

1. _____ 'est-ce que c'est?

2. _____ un stylo.

3. C'est _____ chaise.

4. C'est _____ livre.

F   Écris les lettres qui manquent. *Fill in the missing letters.*

1. pupi___re	9. ___orloge	17. mu___
2. t___bleau	10. ta___lle-crayon	18. sa___le de classe
3. fe___être	11. styl___	19. car___e
4. ___rayon	12. ___raie	20. ___apier
5. gomm___	13. peint___re	21. drape___u
6. ca___ier	14. c___aise	22. poin___e
7. cor___eille à papier	15. burea___	23. r___gle
8. biblioth___que	16. bros___e	24. li___re

Mots croisés

G

Vertical

1. Place to sit.
2. Where light is admitted.
3. Large desk.
4. Source of knowledge.
5. Container for discarded paper.
7. Straight edge.
9. Writing instrument.

Horizontal

3. Storage place for books, manuscripts, and records.
6. Side of a room.
8. Used to erase chalk marks.
10. At end of a pencil.
11. "... de classe."
12. Opposite "une gomme."
13. Important items are listed in this.

VIVEMENT LES VACANCES!

2+2 =

SUISSE

BELGIQUE

LE GRAND LIVRE DU MOIS
vous offre
TOUT DE SUITE
4 livres reliés
pour le prix d'1
plus une montre à quartz soit :

PREMIER LIVRE	
DEUXIEME LIVRE	84 F
TROISIEME LIVRE	GRATUIT
QUATRIEME LIVRE	GRATUIT
	GRATUIT
MONTRE A QUARTZ (Valeur 89,00 F)	15 F

99F
l'ensemble
(port compris)

Sans aucun engagement d'achat au Club.

39F
Miracle économique!

FLIMRICK horloge.
Mouvement à quartz.
Garantie 1 an.
Ø 23 cm. 39F

1. RAFSA

TJI lot de 2 range-revues. Carton ondulé laqué. Noir. 5F

5F/2 pces

▶ Sur la photo
1. RAFSA accessoires de bureau. Acrylique. Corbeille à courrier. 95F Pot à crayons, 45F Range-courrier 55F

▶ Sur la photo
2. PUCK accessoires de bureau. Plastique. Blanc/noir. Ens. 3 range-revues, 3 casiers à courrier, 1 corbeille à papiers. 85F
Ens. 1 range-courrier/ porte-stylo, 1 bloc-notes, 1 boîte à trombones. 35F
3. HÖJDARE range-revues. Carton ondulé. 3 pces. 28F
Casier archives. Contient 12 chemises format A4. 48F
4. TAMP tableau d'affichage magnétique. Métal laqué. 39×45 cm. 38F 79×45 cm. 55F

LOM corbeille à papiers. Divers coloris. 12 litres. 9F

9F

FLIT 2 pces
18F

5. KAOS

5. POPP

6. ORRE

▶ Sur la photo
5. POPP range-revues. Lot de 3. 25F
6. ORRE corbeille à papiers. Acier laqué. Noir ou rouge. 20l. 45F
7. FABIAN étagère et 2 consoles. Noir.
Long. 74 cm. Prof. 24 cm. 45F
8. FLIT serre-livres. Fil laqué époxy. Rouge vif ou noir. La paire. 18F
9. KAOS lot de 5 range-revues. Carton ondulé peint. 40F

▶ Sur la photo
10. BRÅDIS horloge. Aluminium. Mécanisme à quartz. garantie 1 an. Ø 39 cm. 225F
11. DOKUMENT accessoires de bureau. Métal extrudé, laqué époxy noir.
Range-courrier. 30F Sous-main. 65F Ens. corbeille à courrier. 175F Range-revues. 78F Pot à crayons. Les 2 40F Tableau d'affichage 60×90 cm. 145F Range-crayons. 40F Corbeille à papiers. 68F

97F50

CARTABLE
41 x 30 x 12 cm.
Croûte de cuir de porc.
2 soufflets et un compartiment à glissière.
2 poches avant.

Unit 2   Classroom Objects   15

CLASSROOM COMMANDS
Les Ordres donnés en classe

Répète.
Repeat.

Parle.
Speak.

Dis-le en français.
Say it in French.

Complète les phrases.
Complete the sentences.

Réponds à la question.
Answer the question.

Lève la main.
Raise your hand.

Prends une feuille de papier.
Take out paper.

Ouvre le livre.
Open the book.

Ferme le livre.
Close the book.

Écris.
Write.

Écoute.
Listen.

Lis.
Read.

Assieds-toi.
Sit down.
Be seated.

Complète les phrases.
Complete the sentences.

Va au tableau.
Go to the board.

Qui ne dit mot, consent.

Silence is consent.

A Do what your teacher commands.

B Écris en français, s'il te plaît. *Write in French, please.*

1. (Speak.) _____

2. (Say.) _____

3. (Answer.) _____

C Do what the following command tells you to do.

Écris ton nom. _____.

D Match the English with the French.

A		B	
1. répondre _____		a) to read	
2. lever _____		b) to repeat	
3. aller _____		c) to answer	
4. répéter _____		d) to raise	
5. lire _____		e) to go	

E Écris un ordre en français pour chaque illustration. *Write a command in French for each picture.*

1. _____

2. _____

3. _____

4. _____

5. _____

F   Complète chaque phrase en français. *Complete each sentence in French.*

1. _____ la main.

2. Va au _____ .

3. _____ -le en français.

4. Réponds à la _____ .

5. _____ le livre.

6. Prends une feuille de _____ .

7. _____ les phrases.

G   Choose the corresponding command in each group.

1. Complete.   (Va.   Parle.   Complète.)
2. Repeat.   (Répète.   Écris.   Ferme.)
3. Read.   (Ouvre.   Lis.   Écoute.)
4. Listen.   (Écoute.   Écris.   Sors.)
5. Answer.   (Ferme.   Lis.   Réponds.)

MINICOM

TAPEZ 3612

Le service de correspondance par Minitel de France Télécom.

TELECARTE 50

ÉCRIS VITE À LYDIA

ACHETEZ-LE MAINTENANT!

2.00$ DE RABAIS

SUR LES CADRES &/OU ALBUMS

PHONE BOX MUSIC

DEVENEZ UNE STAR DU SHOW-BIZ...
...et gagnez une TWINGO

☎ 36 70 80 07 / 36 68 80 07

Téléphonez d'où ça vous chante.

REJOIGNEZ-NOUS SUR MINITEL

CODE 36-15 PAP

joue et gagne au

BATMAN

36.68.2001

2.19 F/mn

3615 BATMAN

AIR FRANCE

DEMANDEZ-NOUS LE MONDE

4 NUMBERS
Les Nombres

Combien font...?   How many are...?

11 onze
12 douze
13 treize
14 quatorze
15 quinze

1 un
2 deux
3 trois
4 quatre
5 cinq

6 six
7 sept
8 huit
9 neuf
10 dix

16 seize
17 dix-sept
18 dix-huit
19 dix-neuf

20 vingt
21 vingt et un
22 vingt-deux
23 vingt-trois
24 vingt-quatre
25 vingt-cinq
26 vingt-six
27 vingt-sept
28 vingt-huit
29 vingt-neuf

30 trente
31 trente et un
32 trente-deux

40 quarante
41 quarante et un
42 quarante-deux

50 cinquante
51 cinquante et un
52 cinquante-deux

60 soixante
61 soixante et un
62 soixante-deux

70 soixante-dix
71 soixante et onze
72 soixante-douze

80 quatre-vingts
81 quatre-vingt-un
82 quatre-vingt-deux

90 quatre-vingt-dix
91 quatre-vingt-onze
92 quatre-vingt-douze

100 cent
200 deux cents
1000 mille

Un tiens vaut mieux
que deux tu l'auras.

A bird in the hand is
worth two in the bush.

Supplementary Vocabulary

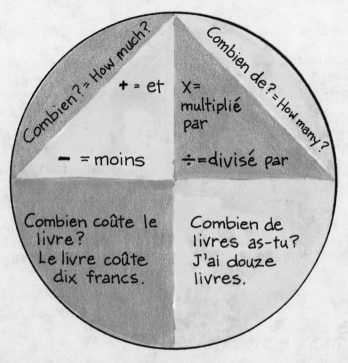

Exercises

A After you have studied the numbers and practiced saying them, try to write these numbers from memory. (En français, s'il te plaît.)

1 _____   6 _____

2 _____   7 _____

3 _____   8 _____

4 _____   9 _____

5 _____   10 _____

B Rate yourself. How did you do? Circle your evaluation.

1. very well   2. fairly well   3. poorly

C Practice again. Écris les nombres.

    EXEMPLE: onze ___11___

1. cinq _____   4. neuf _____

2. huit _____   5. sept _____

3. un _____

D Écris le mot français pour chaque nombre.

4 _____   6 _____

2 _____   8 _____

E Tell whether the following equations indicate addition, subtraction, multiplication, or division.

1. Quatorze divisé par sept font deux. _____

2. Deux et dix font douze. _____

3. Huit multiplié par trois font vingt-quatre. _____

4. Dix-neuf moins treize font six. _____

F Write once more Numbers 1-10. Try not to look at any of the exercises that preceded. (En français, s'il te plaît.)

9 _____   1 _____   6 _____   4 _____   7 _____

2 _____   5 _____   8 _____   3 _____   10 _____

G Combien d'objets sont représentés? *How many objects are pictured? Write the number in French.*

= _____

= _____

= _____

= _____

= _____

H Il y a combien d'objets en tout? *How many objects are there altogether?* _____

Now, write this sum in French. _____

I Écris les réponses en français.

  EXEMPLE: 6 − 4 = <u>deux</u>

1. 12 × 4 = _____

2. 30 − 10 = _____

3. 8 − 6 = _____

4. 12 + 18 = _____

5. 100 ÷ 2 = _____

6. 60 + 10 = _____

7. 30 − 15 = _____

8. 80 ÷ 2 = _____

9. 10 × 10 = _____

10. 15 + 4 = _____

J Your teacher will say ten numbers in French. Write the corresponding numerals.

1. _____ 6. _____

2. _____ 7. _____

3. _____ 8. _____

4. _____ 9. _____

5. _____ 10. _____

K How many interior angles are there in each figure? Circle the number.

quatre
huit
dix
trois

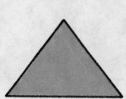

cinq
trois
quatre
sept

sept
six
onze
cinq

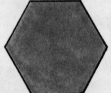

cinq
neuf
huit
onze

L Lis le passage. Choisis les réponses applicables.

La salle de classe est très agréable. Il y a beaucoup d'objets ici: quinze gommes, vingt livres, onze chaises et une corbeille à papier. Une gomme coûte trente-cinq cents. Une chaise coûte quinze dollars. Un livre coûte trois dollars, et une corbeille coûte sept dollars.

1. Il y a beaucoup d'objets dans la salle de classe, n'est-ce pas?
   a) oui   b) non

2. Il y a combien d'objets dans la salle de classe?
   a) quarante-sept   b) quatorze
   c) quatre   d) huit

3. Combien coûte un livre?
   a) $ 3.00   b) $ .03
   c) $30.00   d) $ .13

4. Il y a combien de gommes dans la salle de classe?
   a) trente-cinq   b) six
   c) cinquante   d) quinze

5. Combien coûte une chaise?
   a) $11.00   b) $ .50
   c) $15.00   d) $ 5.00

Mots croisés

M

Vertical

1. (Square root of 16) + 4 = ...
2. To find an average, a total is . . . by the number of items in it.
3. One fourth of a bicentennial = . . . years.
4. (shown as Horizontal)
5. Complete the progression: 0, 20, 40, . . . 80.
6. A bicentennial celebrates . . . years.
7. Thirty plus ten = ...
9. A millenium = . . . years.
11. Twenty percent of 100 = ...
15. Word for the addition sign.

Horizontal

4. The word *times* is . . . in French.
8. Opposite of addition sign.
10. (Square of 2) + 2 = ...
12. Square of ten = ...
13. Two and one half dozen = ...
14. One dozen + one = ...
16. Square root of 9.

DANS LA VIE...

...JE SAIS BIEN QU'UN PLUS UN...

...NE FAIT PAS TOUJOURS DEUX!

MAIS TU POURRAS TOUJOURS COMPTER SUR MOI!

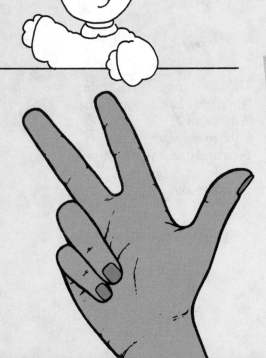

Lunettes de soleil de haut en bas, rouges, vertes, bleues (660 F, 560 F, 580 F, Traction Production chez Hervé Domat), rouges (846 F, Lafont chez Foncalet Opticien), jaunes, vertes et bleues cerclées métal (265 F la paire, Scooter), rondes jaunes et orange (69 F la paire, Bathroom Graffiti).

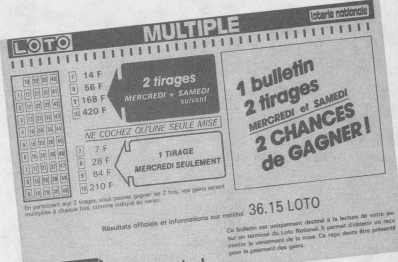

GEOGRAPHY
La Géographie

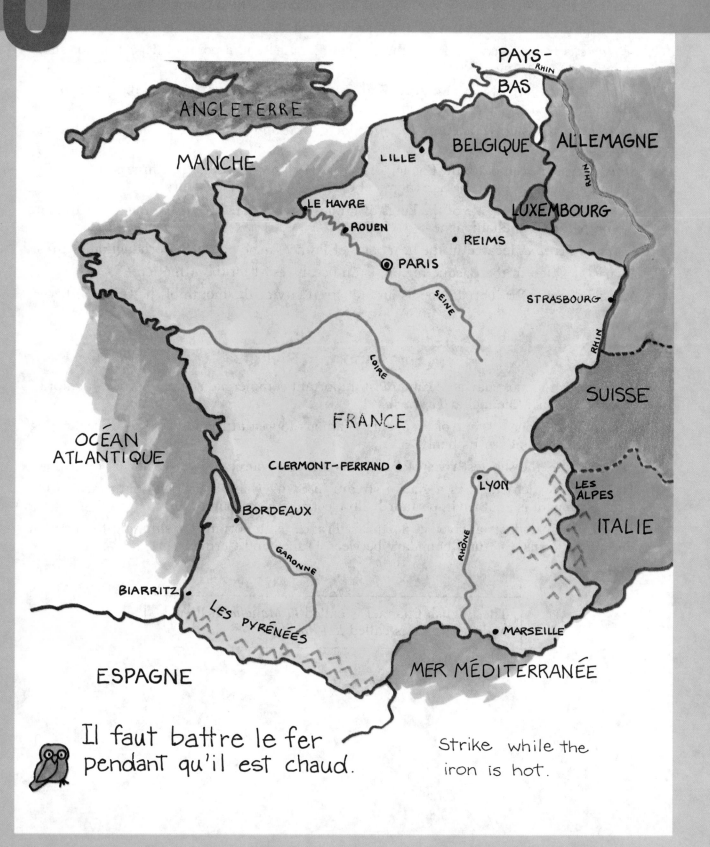

Il faut battre le fer pendant qu'il est chaud.

Strike while the iron is hot.

Important Cities

Paris, an inland port, is the capital of France and its most populated city. It is the economic and cultural center of the nation and an international fashion center.

Marseille, on the Mediterranean, is France's largest seaport and its second largest city.

Le Havre is France's chief port on the English Channel and a point of departure for ships bound for North America.

Lyon, the third largest city of France, is an important commercial city and the center of the silk industry.

Lille, in northeastern France, is a center for cotton and linen fabrics and for industrial machinery.

Strasbourg is the center for the Council of Europe. This river port on the Rhine is noted for its "pâté de foie gras" and the astronomical clock in its Gothic cathedral.

Reims, the coronation site of the kings of France, is also noted for its Gothic cathedral and the preparation of champagne.

Clermont-Ferrand, located in the heart and of France, is noted for the production of tires.

Biarritz, located in the Basque region, is an ocean resort on the Atlantic.

Bordeaux, noted for its red wine, is an industrial city at the mouth of the Garonne River.

Five Important Rivers

The *Seine* is the most navigable and most important commercial river of France. It empties into the English Channel at *Le Havre*.

The *Loire*, the longest river of France, is a famous tourist attraction, due to the charming "châteaux" that adorn its banks.

The *Garonne*, the shortest river of France, is a major source of hydroelectric power.

The *Rhône*, which starts as a glacial stream in Switzerland and flows southward to the Mediterranean, is another important hydroelectric power source.

The *Rhine*, an industrial river in northeast France, is important for shipping to northern Europe. It forms a natural boundary between France and Germany.

> The English Channel is called *la Manche* in French and the Rhine is called *le Rhin*.

A Write the number of each city next to its name.

_____ Biarritz

_____ Clermont-Ferrand

_____ Le Havre

_____ Lille

_____ Lyon

_____ Marseille

_____ Paris

_____ Reims

_____ Strasbourg

_____ Bordeaux

B Identify the cities described in the information below.

1. Ocean resort: _____

2. Cotton and linen fabric center: _____

3. Tire center: _____

4. Silk center: _____

5. Center of the Council of Europe: _____

6. Chief port on the English Channel: _____

7. Most important inland port: _____

8. Coronation site of the kings of France: _____

9. Industrial city on the Garonne River: _____

10. Port on the Mediterranean Sea: _____

C Study the map carefully. Then find the following items.

1. The mountain range separating France from Spain: _____

2. The most important commercial river: _____

3. The ocean bordering France on the west and northwest: _____

4. The country bordering France on the north: _____

5. The longest river of France: _____

D Match Column **B** with Column **A**.

A	B
1. Reims _____	a) international fashion center
2. Strasbourg _____	b) Mediterranean seaport
3. Loire _____	c) port on the English Channel
4. Biarritz _____	d) important silk center
5. Clermont-Ferrand _____	e) cotton and linen center
6. Marseille _____	f) industrial port on the Rhine
7. Lyon _____	g) center for champagne
8. Paris _____	h) tire-producing city
9. Le Havre _____	i) Basque ocean resort
10. Lille _____	j) longest river of France

E Écris le nom de la ville indiquée par l'illustration. *Name the city associated with each picture.*

1. _____

2. _____

3. _____

4. _____

5. _____

F   Choisis la réponse correcte. *Complete each sentence correctly.*

1. The most populated city of France is....
    a) Lille   b) Paris   c) Rouen   d) Marseille

2. The shortest river of France is the....
    a) Seine   b) Rhône   c) Loire   d) Garonne

3. An Atlantic resort city is....
    a) Biarritz   b) Paris   c) Lyon   d) Strasbourg

4. Lyon is noted for its....
    a) cathedral   b) cotton   c) silk   d) linen

5. France's most navigable river is the....
    a) Garonne   b) Seine   c) Loire   d) Rhône

6. A city located in the center of France is....
    a) Paris   b) Le Havre   c) Clermont-Ferrand d) Biarritz

7. Switzerland borders France on the....
    a) east   b) north   c) south   d) west

8. Two major sources of hydroelectric power are the Garonne and the....
    a) Seine   b) Loire   c) Rhône   d) Rhin

9. The Pyrénées separate France from....
    a) Germany   b) Poland   c) Italy   d) Spain

10. The Alps separate France from Switzerland and....
    a) Austria   b) Italy   c) Spain   d) Germany

G Write in each blank space the answer that makes each statement geographically correct.

France is shaped like a hexagon, a six-sided figure. 1._____ sides confront the water, and 2._____ sides have land boundaries. 3._____ sides form boundaries with other countries. The shortest border is with the country of 4._____, and the longest is with 5._____. In addition, two mountain ranges create natural boundaries for France. The 6._____ Mountains separate France from Spain, whereas the 7._____, stretching across central Europe, divide France from Italy and Switzerland.

Of the five major rivers only the 8._____ flows southward. Starting as a glacial stream, it passes through the industrial city of 9._____ and empties into the Mediterranean 10._____. The 11._____ River flows into the English Channel. It is considered France's most 12._____ river. In Paris, merchandise for transoceanic export is either loaded into barges and shipped to 13._____, or transported overland to that city. Another busy commercial river is the 14._____, a natural water border with Germany. Although of minimal value in terms of transportation, the 15._____ is invaluable as a source of hydroelectric power. It begins in the 16._____ Mountains and passes through the busy port city of 17._____. A pleasure cruise down the 18._____ River offers spectacular views of beautiful historic buildings called 19._____. At its mouth, one may leave the boat and take a swim in the 20._____ Ocean.

H Imagine that...

1. you are a French official trying to convince a group of American business people to establish companies in France. List five cities to which you would take the group, and tell why you would take it there.

   _____

   _____

   _____

   _____

   _____

   _____

   _____

   _____

   _____

   _____

2. your family is taking you on a trip to France. Name six places you would enjoy visiting, and tell what you would like to do or see there.

   _____

   _____

   _____

   _____

   _____

   _____

   _____

   _____

   _____

   _____

Maze

Marie-Josette and Michel are ready to travel. Trace their vacation route to find out where they will be spending the summer. Name their destination in the space provided. List the places they will visit while en route.

Places they'll visit:

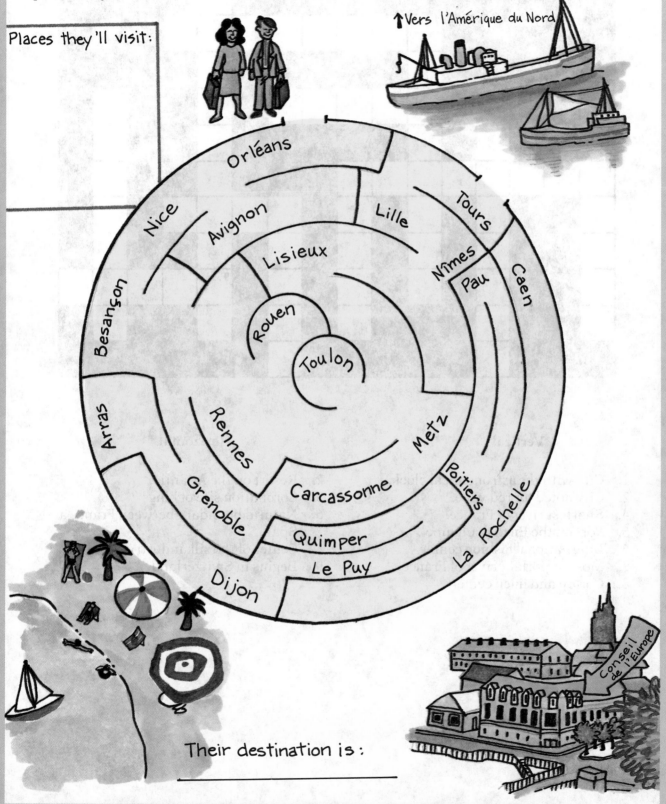

Vers l'Amérique du Nord

Orléans
Nice
Avignon
Lille
Tours
Lisieux
Nîmes
Pau
Caen
Besançon
Rouen
Toulon
Arras
Rennes
Metz
Grenoble
Carcassonne
Poitiers
Quimper
La Rochelle
Le Puy
Dijon

Conseil de l'Europe

Their destination is: _____

Mots croisés

J

Vertical

1. City with the astronomical clock.
2. City noted for red wine.
4. Shortest river of France.
5. Port on the English Channel.
6. International fashion center.
7. Most important river of France.
8. Cotton and linen center.

Horizontal

2. Resort on the Atlantic.
3. Coronation site of kings.
6. Natural boundary between France and Spain.
8. Center of the silk industry.
9. Begins in Switzerland.

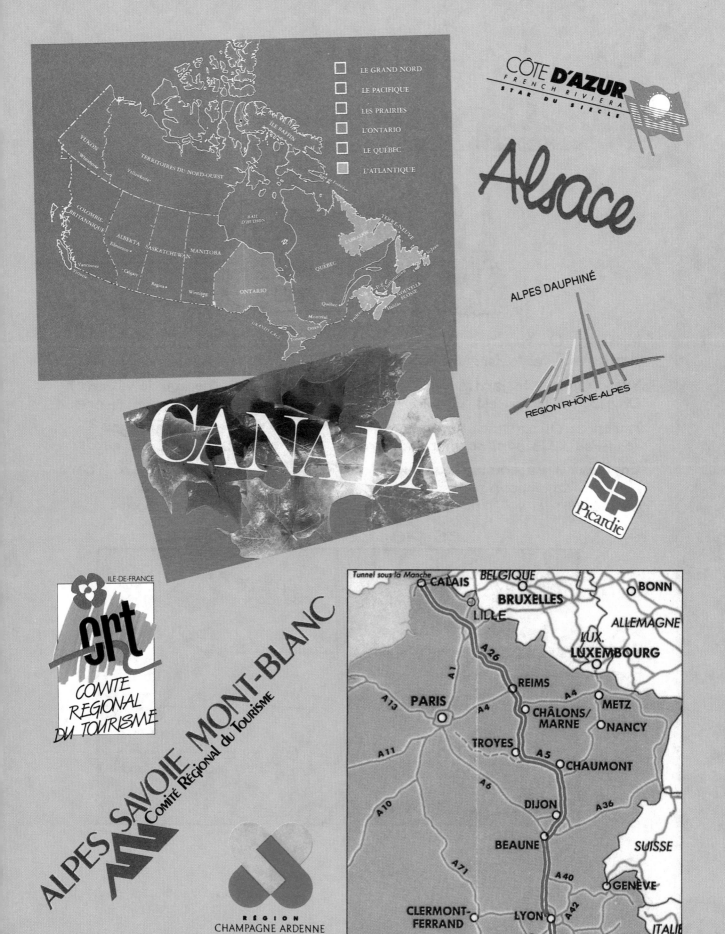

LE GRAND NORD

LE PACIFIQUE

LES PRAIRIES

L'ONTARIO

LE QUÉBEC

L'ATLANTIQUE

CÔTE D'AZUR
FRENCH RIVIERA
STAR DU SIECLE

Alsace

ALPES DAUPHINÉ

RÉGION RHÔNE-ALPES

CANADA

Picardie

ILE-DE-FRANCE

crt
COMITÉ
RÉGIONAL
DU TOURISME

ALPES SAVOIE MONT-BLANC
COMITÉ RÉGIONAL DU TOURISME

RÉGION
CHAMPAGNE ARDENNE

Tunnel sous la Manche

BELGIQUE
CALAIS
BRUXELLES
BONN
LILLE
ALLEMAGNE
A26
LUX.
A1
LUXEMBOURG
REIMS
A4
METZ
PARIS
A4
CHÂLONS/
MARNE
NANCY
A13
TROYES
A5
CHAUMONT
A11
A6
DIJON
A36
A10
BEAUNE
SUISSE
A71
A40
GENÈVE
CLERMONT-
FERRAND
LYON
A42
ITALIE
ST-ÉTIENNE
A7

6 HOUSE
La Maison

Monique: Où habites-tu?	Where do you live?
Maryvonne: J'habite dans une maison à Lyon.	I live in a house in Lyon.
Yves: Où est le jardin?	Where is the garden (yard)?
Olivier: Le jardin est là-bas.	The garden is over there.
Florence: Où sont les garages?	Where are the garages?
Jean-Paul: Ils sont derrière le jardin.	They are behind the garden.
Sophie: Il y a combien de pièces dans ta maison?	How many rooms are there in your house?
Guillaume: Il y a cinq pièces.	There are five rooms.

Les pièces de la maison

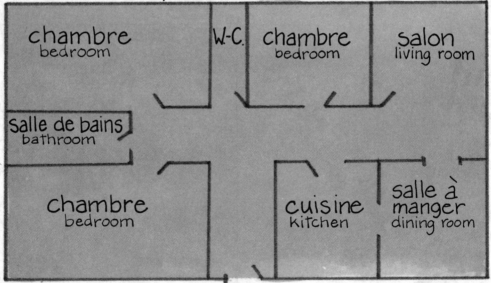

chambre
bedroom

W-C.

chambre
bedroom

salon
living room

Salle de bains
bathroom

chambre
bedroom

cuisine
kitchen

salle à manger
dining room

 Nécessité fait loi.   Necessity is its own law.

38

Supplementary Vocabulary

1. château

2. maison individuelle

3. résidence, immeuble

4. appartement

5. caravane, roulotte

6. hutte

7. tente

A Écris le français pour chaque pièce.

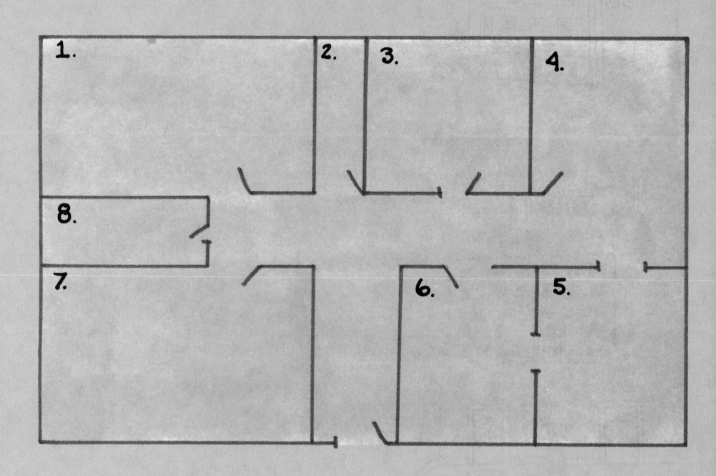

B Complète les phrases.

1. Je <u>fais la cuisine</u> dans la _____.
      (cook)

2. Je <u>mange</u> dans la _____.
      (eat)

3. Je <u>me couche</u> dans la _____.

4. Je <u>me lave</u> dans la _____.
      (wash)

5. Je <u>joue</u> dans le _____.
      (play)

6. Je <u>me distrais</u> dans le _____.
      (relax)

C Choisis la pièce correcte.

1. salle à manger   (bedroom   kitchen   dining room)
2. cuisine   (bathroom   kitchen   bedroom)
3. chambre   (bedroom   bathroom   living room)
4. salle de bains   (bathroom   kitchen   bedroom)
5. salon   (living room   bathroom   dining room)

D In which room would you find (en français, s'il te plaît)...

1. a dining table? _____

2. a refrigerator? _____

3. an alarm clock? _____

4. a piano? _____

5. a shower? _____

E Complète chaque phrase en français.

1. A house towed by a car is a _____.

2. A building housing many families is a _____.

3. An expensive large country house is a _____.

4. Scouts learn how to pitch a _____.

5. The kitchen, bedroom, and bathroom are rooms of the _____.

F Écris les mots correctement. *Unscramble the words.*

1. nomsia _____

2. bramche _____

3. nalso _____

4. inisuce _____

5. abnis _____

MAISON   FAMILLE   AMOUR

G   Lis le passage. Complète chaque phrase correctement.

Ma maison est belle. J'habite ici avec ma famille. J'aime ma maison et ma famille. Ma maison a cinq pièces. Le jardin est derrière la maison.

1. Ma maison est . . . .
   a) combien
   b) belle
   c) nouvelle
   d) grande

2. J'habite . . . .
   a) avec mes parents
   b) à Paris
   c) derrière le jardin
   d) dans le garage

3. Derrière la maison est . . . .
   a) le jardin
   b) la maison
   c) la famille
   d) la pièce

4. La maison a . . . pièces.
   a) huit
   b) sept
   c) six
   d) cinq

H

Vertical

1. Guests are received in the....
2. The car's house.
3. « . . . le jardin? » (*Where is*)
4. Family dwelling.
5. Where one sleeps.
7. Where food is prepared.

Horizontal

4. "Salle à . . . ."
6. « . . . fait loi. »
8. One washes oneself in the "salle de . . . ."
9. One resides here.
10. Outdoor recreational area.
11. Camping shelter.

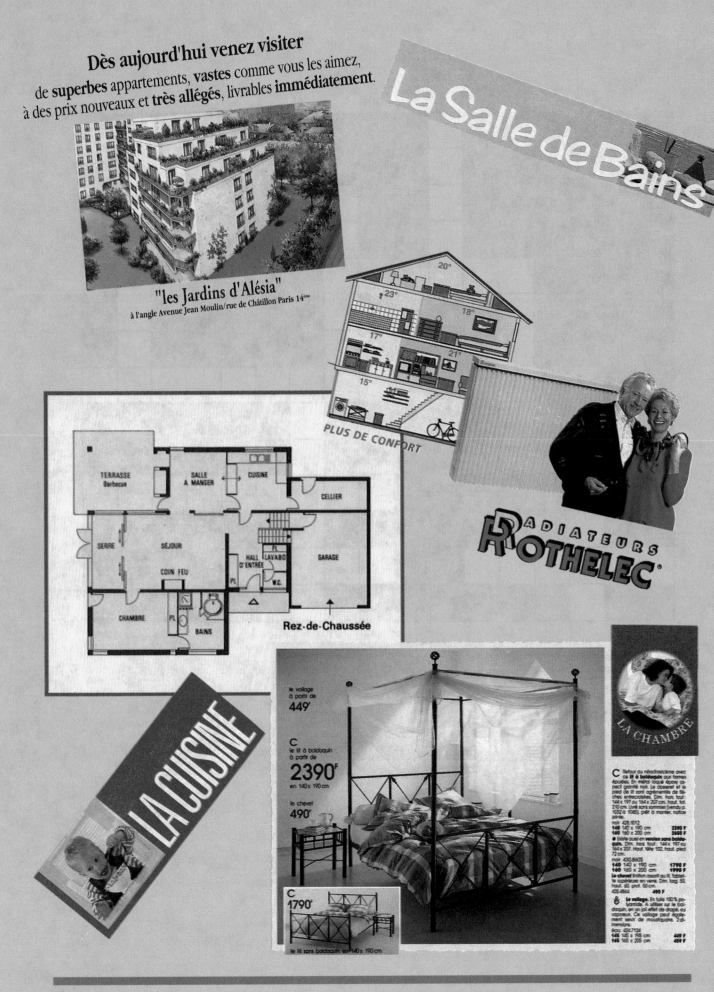

Dès aujourd'hui venez visiter
de **superbes** appartements, **vastes** comme vous les aimez, à des prix nouveaux et très **allégés**, livrables **immédiatement**.

"les Jardins d'Alésia"
à l'angle Avenue Jean Moulin/rue de Châtillon Paris 14ème

La Salle de Bains

PLUS DE CONFORT

RADIATEURS ROTHELEC

Rez-de-Chaussée

LA CUISINE

LA CHAMBRE

le voilage à partir de **449ᶠ**

C le lit à baldaquin à partir de **2390ᶠ** en 140 x 190 cm

le chevet **490ᶠ**

C **1790ᶠ**
le lit sans baldaquin en 140 x 190 cm

FAMILY
La Famille

Véronique: Qui est-ce ?
Bertrand: C'est mon <u>frère</u>.

Jean-Marcel : Qui sont les enfants ?
Anne: Ce sont ma <u>petite-fille</u> et mon <u>petit-fils</u>.

Françoise: Ce sont tes <u>parents</u> ?
Jacques : Oui, ma <u>mère</u> s'appelle Brigitte, et mon <u>père</u> s'appelle Luc.

Claire: Denise, Jeanne et Patrice sont soeurs et frère, n'est-ce pas ?
Bernard: Oui, et ce sont aussi mes cousins.

Who is this?
It's my <u>brother</u>.

Who are the children?
They're my <u>granddaughter</u> and my <u>grandson</u>.

Are they your <u>parents</u>?
Yes, my <u>mother</u>'s name is Brigitte, and my <u>father</u>'s name is Luc.

Denise, Jeanne and Patrice are sisters and brother, aren't they?
Yes, and they are also my cousins.

N'oublie pas:
Réunion de famille
Les invités
• grand-père , grand-mère
• Tante Louise et son mari
• Cousine Yvette
• Cousin Étienne
• ma soeur et ses enfants
• André et sa femme
• Catherine et le bébé

Don't forget:
Family Reunion
Guests
• grandfather, grandmother
• Aunt Louise and her husband
• Cousin Yvette
• Cousin Etienne
• my sister and her children
• André and his wife
• Catherine and the baby

Pierre: Où sont tes <u>parents</u> ?
Marie: Mes <u>grands-parents</u> sont à l'intérieur, et mes oncles et mes tantes sont dans le jardin.

Antoinette: Ta <u>marraine</u> et ton <u>parrain</u>, sont-ils ici ?
Paul: Bien sûr. Ma <u>marraine</u> parle avec mes tantes. Mon <u>parrain</u> est sur la terrasse.

Marcelle: Comment s'appellent ton <u>neveu</u> et ta <u>nièce</u>?
Hervé : Mon neveu s'appelle Michel, et ma nièce s'appelle Constance.

Annette: Tu es leur <u>oncle</u> unique?
René : Non, Robert est aussi leur oncle.

Where are your <u>relatives</u>?
My <u>grandparents</u> are inside, and my uncles and aunts are in the garden.

Are your <u>godparents</u> here?
Yes, of course. My <u>godmother</u> is speaking with my aunts. My <u>godfather</u> is on the terrace.

What are the names of your <u>nephew</u> and <u>niece</u>?
My nephew's name is Michel, and my niece's name is Constance.

Are you their only <u>uncle</u>?
No, Robert is also their uncle.

Tel père, tel fils.

Like father, like son.

la jeune fille
the girl

l'enfant
the child

le garçon
the boy

la fille
the daughter

le fils
the son

la femme
the woman, wife

l'homme
the man

le (m. sing.) = the
la (f. sing.) = the

les (m. & f. pl.) = the

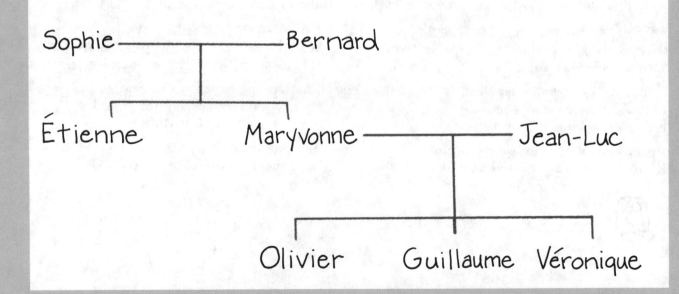

Sophie ——————— Bernard

Étienne   Maryvonne ——————— Jean-Luc

Olivier   Guillaume   Véronique

Exercises

A Indicate Véronique's relationship to each family member listed.

Véronique est la

1. _____ de Guillaume.
2. _____ de Maryvonne.
3. _____ de Bernard.
4. _____ d'Olivier.
5. _____ de Sophie.
6. _____ d'Étienne.
7. _____ de Jean-Luc.

B Fais la même chose pour Maryvonne et Bernard. *Then, do the same thing for Maryvonne and Bernard.*

Maryvonne est la

1. _____ de Guillaume, d'Olivier et de Véronique.
2. _____ de Jean-Luc.
3. _____ d'Étienne.
4. _____ de Bernard et de Sophie.

Bernard est le

1. _____ de Véronique, de Guillaume et d'Olivier.
2. _____ d'Étienne et de Maryvonne.
3. _____ de Sophie.

C Qui est-ce? *Who is this?* (En français, s'il te plaît.)

1. Sœur de ma mère: _____
2. Fils de ma tante: _____
3. Père de ma mère: _____
4. Fille de mon frère: _____
5. Père de ma sœur: _____

D Qui suis-je? *Who am I?* (En français, s'il te plaît.)

1. I am your father's son. In other words, I am your _____.
2. I am your niece's mother. In other words, I am your _____.
3. I am your brother's son. In other words, I am your _____.
4. I am your mother's father. In other words, I am your _____.

E Choisis la réponse correcte. *Choose the correct response.*

1. Où sont les grands-parents?
   a) on the bench
   b) in the playpen
   c) in the foreground

2. Où sont les parents?
   a) on the bench
   b) in the playpen
   c) in the foreground

3. Où est l'enfant?
   a) on the bench
   b) in the playpen
   c) in the foreground

F   Écris en anglais.

1. Qui est-ce? _____

2. Qui suis-je? _____

3. Qui est le frère? _____

4. Qui arrive? _____

G   Complète en français.

1. Qui est le garçon? *(son)*
   C'est mon _____ .

2. Qui est la femme? *(mother)*
   C'est ma _____ .

3. Qui est l'homme? *(uncle)*
   C'est mon _____ .

H   Lis le passage. Écris le passage en anglais.

Ma famille

Ma famille habite[1] à Louvain. Elle n'est ni grande ni[2] petite. Il y a quatre personnes. Mon frère a quinze ans, et j'ai onze ans. Mes parents sont professeurs. Nous habitons dans une jolie[3] maison.

_____

_____

_____

_____

_____

[1]**habiter** = to live, reside   [2]**ne** . . . **ni** . . . **ni** = neither . . . nor   [3]**jolie** = pretty

TU ES LA MAMAN DE MES RÊVES ...

Infatigable,

Adorable,

Admirable,

Irréprochable...

... vraiment formidable !

Joyeux Anniversaire !

THÉÂTRE DE 10 HEURES 46 06 10 17
20h30
les
jeunes
pères
d'après le guide du jeune père
Mise en scène
Philippe
Ferran
avec
Philippe Rouiller
et Henri Falloux

Sylvie et David

Vous invitent à partager leur joie
en participant ou en vous unissant d'intention
à la célébration de leur mariage

Le Samedi 25 Septembre 1993, à 16 heures
en l'église reformée, 12, rue Guérin
Charenton-le-Pont

POUR ENFANTS CHOC
choisissez le CHIC des « ENFANTS
TERRIBLES ».
Salopette Trotinette, 12 mois, 409 F.
LES ENFANTS TERRIBLES, 7 rue Fondeau
Montpellier 67.52.96.81.

adoptions

**Bernard et Catherine
PÉROT**
laissent à Antoine
la joie d'annoncer l'arrivée
de
Clémence

née à Bangkok,
le 30 juillet 1990.
44, rue Laetitia,
92500 Rueil-Malmaison.

JUSQU'À
12
ANS
**150
ACTIVITES
POUR VOS
PETITS-
ENFANTS**
RETZ

**Barbecues à pierres de lave
Camping Gaz®, pour que les bons moments
soient simplement meilleurs.**

50

OCCUPATIONS
Les Professions et les Métiers

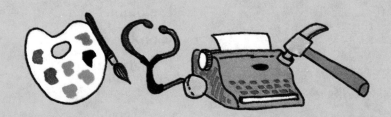

Quelle est ta profession?
Je suis <u>acteur</u>.
Que fais-tu?
Je suis <u>actrice</u>.

What is your profession?
I'm an <u>actor</u>.
What do you do (for a living)?
I am an actress.

artiste (m.&f.) = artist
professeur (m.) = teacher (man or woman)
médecin (m.) = physician (man or woman)
Commerçant = storekeeper
commerçante = storekeeper
facteur (m.) = letter carrier

Bureau de placement Acme
On cherche:

charpentier (m.)   plombier (m.)
cuisinier, -ière   électricien (m.)
infirmier, -ière   mécanicien, -ienne
fermier, -ière   musicien, -ienne

Emploi garanti

Tel. 12-59-43

Acme Employment Agency
Wanted:

carpenter   plumber
cook   electrician
nurse   mechanic
farmer   musician

Work guaranteed

Tel. 12-59-43

 À force de forger on
devient forgeron.

Practice makes perfect.

Exercises

A Number in order the professions or trades as your teacher recites them.

le facteur _____   la musicienne _____

le médecin _____   l'artiste _____

le commerçant _____   le plombier _____

la cuisinière _____   le professeur _____

le fermier _____   le charpentier _____

B Qui travaille ici? *Who works here?*

1. Restaurant: _____

2. Wood shop: _____

3. Post office: _____

4. School: _____

5. Garage: _____

6. Dairy barn: _____

7. Stage: _____

8. Hospital: _____

9. Sales office: _____

10. Studio: _____

C Écris les mots correctement.

1. ruteca _____

2. dicemén _____

3. ratcuef _____

4. tarseti _____

5. birepoml _____

D Write the sentences in English. Look first, then take a good guess.

1. Ma mère est interprète.

   _____

2. Elle parle allemand et espagnol.

   _____

3. Mon père est musicien.

   _____

4. Il joue de la flûte.

   _____

5. Ma cousine est politicienne.

   _____

6. Elle fait un discours.

   _____

7. Mon cousin est cuisinier.

   _____

8. Il prépare la cuisine.

   _____

E Guess who... (En français, s'il te plaît.)

1. "Le _____" instructs classes.

2. "L' _____" checks for faulty wiring.

3. "Le _____" installs water pipes.

4. "L' _____" paints portraits.

5. "La _____" plants and harvests.

6. "L' _____ *(m.)* _____" assists the physician with patients.

7. "La _____" plays in a symphony orchestra.

8. "Le _____" manages a company.

9. "Le _____" delivers mail.

10. "Le _____" repairs machinery.

F   Écris la profession ou le métier convenable pour chaque illustration.

1.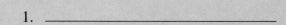

2.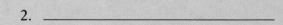

3.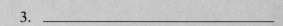

4.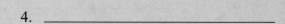

5. _____

- **Patricia Feray**
- 26 ans
- Sans profession
- Le Havre (76)

- **Brigitte Lucia**
- 39 ans
- Secrétaire
- Strasbourg (67)

- **Raymond Denysse**
- 47 ans
- Vendeur de journaux
- Paris (XIII°)

- **Pascal Crapon**
- 33 ans
- Photographe
- Reims (51)

- **René Rabier**
- Retraité
- 70 ans
- Reims (51)

- **Laurence Knittel**
- 22 ans
- Diététicienne
- Thouars (Deux-Sèvres)

- **Aurida Yaïche**
- 20 ans
- Etudiante
- Ivry (Val-de-Marne)

- **Thierry Bianchi**
- 36 ans
- Comptable
- Paris XV°

- **Madeleine Neyhouser**
- 36 ans
- Professeur de lettres
- Metz (Moselle)

- **Madeleine Renaud**
- 55 ans
- Employée à la Poste
- Château-Thierry (Ain)

La médecine est
votre art
et l'écriture
votre
don...

Grand groupe
international du
secteur santé
recrute pour son
siège parisien un

Médecin

Jardin secret ou passion
publique, votre talent et votre
plume sont indissociables de votre
exercice de la médecine.

Maux et mots, vous avez appris à les
distinguer, à en connaître les nuances et
la force.

Loin des modes et des artifices, votre style
nourri de fortes références culturelles sait
plaire, convaincre et raconter la vie.

Si votre don et votre art sont en quête de
nouveaux horizons, cette entreprise du secteur de la
santé saura peut-être leur redonner le goût des
grands espaces.

Une double formation (médecine +
lettres/philo) sera très appréciée.
Merci de nous adresser votre dossier complet
(lettre manuscrite, CV, photo et témoignages
de votre talent) sous référence 648 à RSCG
CARRIERES - 10, rue du Plâtre - 75004
PARIS qui nous le transmettra.

Challengers de demain !

CRÉDIT AGRICOLE DU MIDI

FOOD
La Nourriture

Qu'est-ce qu'il y a à manger?	What are we having to eat?
Il y a de la salade.	We're having salad.
As-tu faim?	Are you hungry?
Oui. J'ai faim.	Yes. I'm hungry.
As-tu soif?	Are you thirsty?
Non. Je n'ai pas soif.	No. I'm not thirsty.

L'Épicerie de Patrice
vente de boissons

FF 15,00	café "caribe" (½ kg)
7,00	thé (½ kg)
3,00	lait (1 litre)
6,00	chocolat en poudre
5,00	eau minérale (2 litres)
6,50	jus de fruit (en boîte)

Patrick's Grocery
beverage sale

"Caribe" coffee (½ kg)	FF 15.00
Tea (½ kg)	7.00
milk (1 liter)	3.00
chocolate powder mix	6.00
mineral water (2 liters)	5.00
fruit juice (can)	6.50

Le Coin de Jeannette
cuisine régionale

Menu du jour — Vendredi

Petit déjeuner
FB 10,00 1."Européen" avec jus
FB 20,00 2. "Fermier"
Deux oeufs, jambon
ou saucisson, pain
grillé, pommes de
terre rôties, boisson
Un bon prix!

Joanie's Corner
regional food

Menu of the Day — Friday

Breakfast
1."Continental" with juice FB 10.00
2."Farmer"   FB 20.00
Two eggs, ham
or sausage, toast,
roast potatoes,
beverage
A real bargain!

 L'appétit vient en mangeant.

The more you have, the more you want.

orange

poire

ananas

pomme

banane

FRUITS

Liste d'achats Shopping List

épinards   spinach
  bifteck   steak
  biscuits   cookies
pommes de terre potatoes
  tomates   tomatoes
  poulet   chicken
  fromage   cheese
  pain   bread
  pudding   pudding
  glace   ice cream

breakfast = petit déjeuner
lunch, midday }
main meal   } déjeuner

supper (light) = souper
supper (main meal) = dîner

"Bon appétit !" — a wish on the part of a friend or host
that all the guests may enjoy the meal and eat heartily

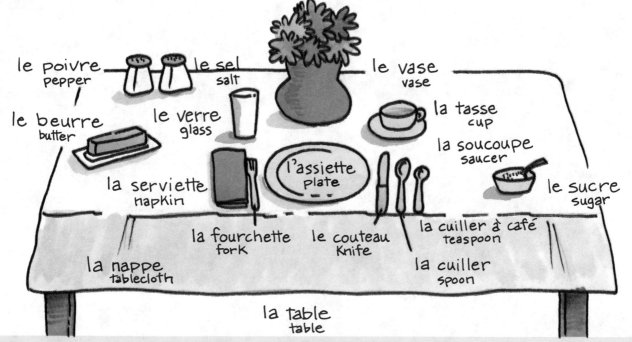

le poivre / pepper

le sel / salt

le vase / vase

le beurre / butter

le verre / glass

la tasse / cup

la soucoupe / saucer

l'assiette / plate

le sucre / sugar

la serviette / napkin

la fourchette / fork

le couteau / knife

la cuiller à café / teaspoon

la nappe / tablecloth

la cuiller / spoon

la table / table

Specialties of France

Escargots — snails prepared with a butter mixture, covered with bread crumbs and baked

Coq au Vin — chicken cooked in a skillet with wine, chicken broth, onions, mushrooms, and spices, and served with potatoes

Canard à l'Orange — roast duck flavored with orange marmalade, vinegar, and soy sauce

Pâté de Foie Gras — pork and goose liver pâté; specialty of Strasbourg

Quiche Lorraine — egg custard pastry filled with bacon, onions, and cheese; specialty of Lorraine

Crêpes Suzette — thin pancakes folded in quarters, served with a flaming sauce of orange juice and sweetened spirits

Éclair — long puff pastry filled with cream or custard and covered with icing

Pot au Feu — beef soup of vegetables and bouillon

French Onion Soup — light golden soup made with consommé, onions, and grated cheese

Bouillabaisse — chowder of various kinds of fish, shellfish and spices, served in a bread-lined soup tureen; specialty of Marseille

Exercises

A Écris le mot français pour chaque objet.

1. _____

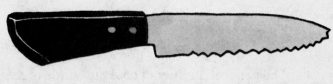

2. _____

3. _____

4. _____

5. _____

6. _____

B Complète chaque phrase en anglais.

1. Two celebrated poultry dishes are _____ and

   _____.

2. The principal ingredients of "bouillabaisse" are _____

   and _____.

3. "Pâté de foie gras" is a specialty of the city of _____.

4. The general manner of cooking snails is _____.

5. A dish consisting of flaming pancakes is _____.

C Write three items for each of the following categories.

meat

1. _____
2. _____
3. _____

beverages

1. _____
2. _____
3. _____

vegetables

1. _____
2. _____
3. _____

fruits

1. _____
2. _____
3. _____

dairy products

1. _____
2. _____
3. _____

desserts

1. _____
2. _____
3. _____

D

Projects

Answer 1 or 2 *and* 3 or 4.

1. You are opening a restaurant in France. From your food list prepare a menu for lunch and dinner. At least three dishes for each meal should be offered. Specialty dishes may be used.
2. Prepare a poster from magazine pictures. Show a balanced breakfast and a balanced dinner. Label each food item with its French name.
3. Prepare fifteen different flashcards with a picture of a food item on one side and its French name on the other.
4. List in French fifteen words that name a food item. Then scramble each word. These can be used in classroom games.
   EXAMPLE: LAIT = TAIL
   SALADE = DAELSA

Mots croisés

E

Vertical

1. Regional dish from Lorraine.
2. « J'ai . . . (*hungry*). »
3. "canard . . . ."
5. Vegetable beef soup.
6. Puffy, iced, cream pastries.
8. Served "à l'orange."
10. Crepes served with an orange sauce.
11. « Bon . . . ! »
12. Thin pancakes.

Horizontal

4. Fisherman's chowder.
5. Liver delicacy.
7. . . . onion soup.
9. Breaded baked snails.
12. Popular beverage.
13. Principal ingredient of French onion soup *(in the singular)*.
14. Necessary to make tea or coffee.

Gâteau au chocolat

Les nourritures à risque

pour les patients allergiques aux aliments

Porc 15% · Pomme de terre 14% · Céleri 35% · Orobe 31%
Arachide 18% · Carotte 6% · Lait de vache, tomate 25%
Blanc d'œuf 29% · Persil · Graine de blé, petits pois 16% · Levure de bière 17% · Orange 18%

COUTEAUX STEACK
le lot de 3
12 F00

PECHES JAUNES
Cal. A - France
le kg
7 F95

POULET ROTI *
le kg
25 F80

TOMATES
Cal. 57
France ou Import
le kg
5 F95

CAMEMBERT
45% M.G.
Montorval
la pièce de 250 g
soit le kg : 27.80 F
6 F95

RESTAURANT
AUX ANCIENS CANADIENS
CUISINE QUÉBÉCOISE FRANÇAISE

Salle à dîner de style typiquement québécois,
aménagée dans la maison Jacquet datant de 1675.
A deux pas du Château Frontenac.
Salles privées pour groupes de 10 à 45 personnes.
Menus spéciaux sur demande.
Réservation recommandée. Cartes de crédit acceptées.
34, rue St-Louis, Québec
(418) 692-1627 · (418) 694-0253

ARTICHAUT
PRINCE DE BRETAGNE
EN COROLLE

Préparation : 15 mn
Cuisson : 45 mn dans une
casserole ou 20 mn en
cocotte-minute

Ingrédients pour 4 personnes :
4 artichauts Prince de Bretagne,
4 œufs, œufs de lump noirs,
persil, sel et poivre.

Après avoir cassé leurs queues, lavez les artichauts dans une eau
vinaigrée. Faites-les cuire comme expliqué précédemment. Égouttez-
les et laissez-les refroidir. Écartez les feuilles extérieures pour former
une corolle. Enlevez le cône des feuilles centrales et le foin en les
faisant pivoter sous une légère pression. Préparez 4 œufs au plat que
vous faites ensuite glisser sur les fonds de chaque artichaut. Disposez
des œufs de lump sur le pourtour des œufs puis poivrez, salez et
décorez avec du persil selon votre goût.

Une vitamine...
«D» vitamines!
MANQUEZ PAS
LE MEILLEUR !
LE LAIT

HARICOTS
VERTS FINS
France
le kg
14 F95

ART
L'Art

Three Great Artists

Jacques Louis David (1748–1825) was born in Paris and studied art under François Boucher. After winning the Prix de Rome in 1775, he was painter to the court of Louis XVI. Napoleon also recognized David's talent and appointed him his court painter. This appointment was surprising because David had opposed Napoleon and had supported the republic. The clear line, chiseled form, and classical themes soon established David the leader of the French neoclassical school. His masterpiece *The Death of Socrates* is an example of his neoclassical style.

Eugène Delacroix (1798–1863) was born near Paris. He studied art in the capital under Pierre Guérin. Delacroix believed that the neoclassists had removed feeling from art, making it as cold and as barren as a petrified forest. To remedy this situation, Delacroix and his romantic school of painters used the flowing line to show motion, coloration and tone to portray feeling, and color contrasts to produce vitality. Delacroix believed that a painting must not only be viewed, it must be felt. *Fantasia arabe* is a masterpiece of this artist.

Édouard Manet (1832–83) was born in Paris and studied art under Thomas Couture. He was one of the founders of the French school of impressionism and one of its best artists. He believed that the painting should create an impression on the viewer. This impression then becomes the viewer's real impression. This type of art uses ghost effect, blending and merging of color, and the joining of background with foreground. *The Croquet Match* and *On the Beach*, two masterpieces of Manet, are striking examples of this style of art.

 Autres temps, autres mœurs.   Different times, different styles.

The Death of Socrates (1787)
by Jacques Louis David
The Metropolitan Museum of Art, New York
(Wolfe Fund, 1931.
Catharine Lorillard Wolfe Collection.)

Fantasia arabe (1853)
by Eugène Delacroix
Städelsches Kunstinstitut, Frankfurt

The Croquet Match (1873)
by Édouard Manet
Städelsches Kunstinstitut, Frankfurt

On the Beach (1873)
by Édouard Manet
Cliché des Musées Nationaux, Paris

Exercises

A Name the picture that shows:

1. people playing an outdoor game. _____

2. a man surrounded by many people. _____

3. a man watching a horseman charge by. _____

B Name the French artist whose works reveal:

1. a clear line and classical themes. _____

2. the flowing line and contrasting color. _____

3. a shadow or ghost effect. _____

4. coloration and tone to portray feeling. _____

5. a blending and merging of color. _____

C Match column B with column A.

A	B
1. Paris _____	a) outstanding romantic painting
2. *Death of Socrates* _____	b) background absorbing foreground
3. Delacroix _____	c) birthplace of David
4. French impressionist _____	d) masterpiece of David
5. *Fantasia arabe* _____	e) Édouard Manet
6. A technique of impressionists _____	f) French romantic artist

D Complete the analogies.

1. _____ : classicism = Delacroix: romanticism

2. David: straight line = Delacroix: _____ line

3. the impression: _____ = reality: David

4. emotion: _____ = form: David

66

E Match the name with the illustration.

Delacroix

Manet

David

F Which artist would most likely be:

1. observing a plastic-covered flower vase? _____

2. painting a firm, noble, and dignified face? _____

3. showing pain in the face of a lost child? _____

G In your opinion,

1. whose representations are as strong as the people they portray?

_____

2. whose paintings illustrate what seems to be happening?

_____

3. whose paintings reveal how his characters feel?

_____

H Which of the paintings in this unit do you like the best? _____

Who painted this masterpiece? _____

State in your own words what the picture is about and why you like it.

_____

_____

_____

_____

_____

_____

_____

I Complète avec les mots qui manquent.

1. _____ was one of the founders of impressionism.

2. _____ was a court painter.

3. Delacroix believed that art should portray _____.

COURS TÉLÉVISÉS
EN
HISTOIRE DE L'ART

Introduction à la peinture
moderne

La peinture moderne
au Québec

Université de Montréal
Faculté des arts et des sciences
Département d'histoire de l'art

LES MODERNES
1870 - 1950

Reliefs
Pierre et lumière

à 19 km de **Paris**

Le Musée national
de la **Renaissance**

au château d'**Ecouen**

Château d'Ecouen - 95440 ECOUEN - Tél. (1) 39 90 04 04
Ouvert tous les jours sauf le mardi de 9h45 à 12h30 et de 14h à 17h15

LES BOURGEOIS DE CALAIS - 1884 - 1895

N° 0079032

MUSÉE RODIN
77, rue de Varenne, 75007 PARIS

LES MODERNES

PARTS OF
THE BODY
Les Parties du corps

la tête

le cou

l'épaule

le coude

la poitrine

le bras

l'estomac

la main

la jambe

le genou

le pied

Mains froides, cœur chaud.   Cold hands but warm heart.

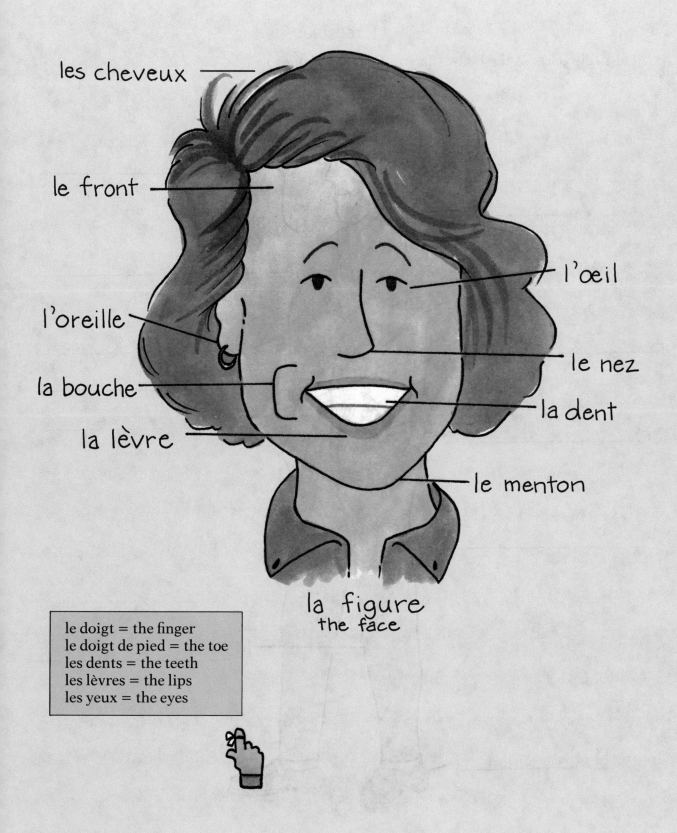

les cheveux

le front

l'oreille

la bouche

la lèvre

l'œil

le nez

la dent

le menton

la figure
the face

le doigt = the finger
le doigt de pied = the toe
les dents = the teeth
les lèvres = the lips
les yeux = the eyes

Exercises

A Label the parts of the body. (En français, s'il te plaît.)

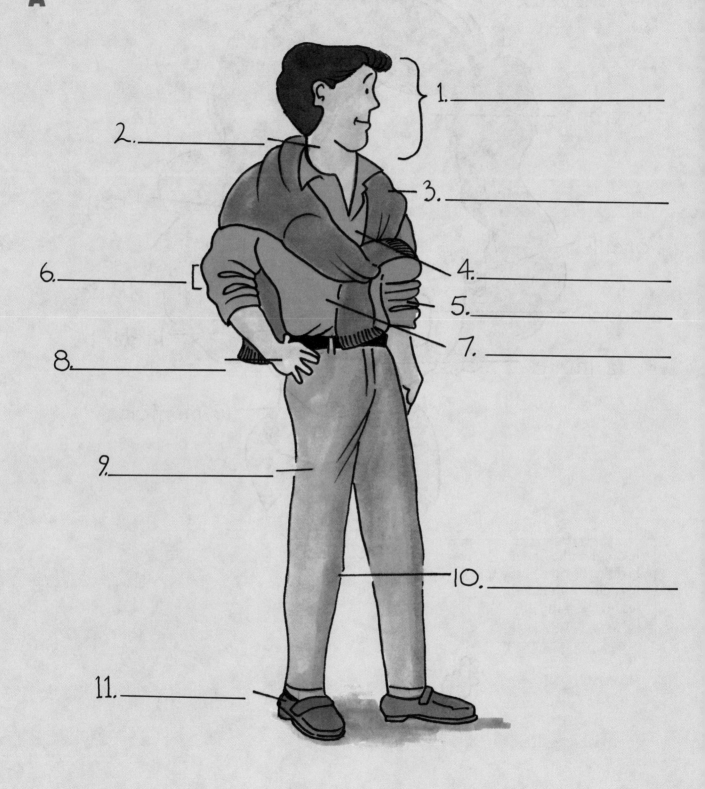

1. _____
2. _____
3. _____
4. _____
5. _____
6. _____
7. _____
8. _____
9. _____
10. _____
11. _____

B Label the parts of the face. (En français, s'il te plaît.)

1._____

2._____

3._____

4._____

5._____

6._____

7._____

8._____

9._____

C Complete the analogies.

1. les lèvres: la bouche = _____: la tête

2. _____: le bras = le pied: la jambe

3. le genou: la jambe = _____: le bras

D Complète chaque phrase en français.

1. We see with our _____.

2. The tongue is in the _____.

3. An _____ is necessary for hearing.

4. The pen is held in the _____.

5. The _____ are needed to chew food.

6. The toes are found on the _____.

7. We use the _____ to smell a rose.

8. We play a guitar with our _____.

9. To hurt your funny bone you must strike your _____.

10. If you eat too much, your _____ will hurt.

E Guess the meaning of the underlined verbs.

1. Je <u>sens</u> avec le nez. _____

2. Je <u>vois</u> avec les yeux. _____

3. Je <u>touche</u> avec les doigts. _____

4. J' <u>entends</u> avec les oreilles. _____

5. Je <u>parle</u> avec la bouche. _____

F   Name the part of the body associated with each illustration. (En français, s'il te plaît.)

1. _____

2. _____

3. _____

Quelle idée!

4. _____

5. _____

6. _____

7. _____

8. _____

9. _____

10. _____

G Match column B with column A.

A	B
1. main _____	a) running
2. pied _____	b) smelling
3. yeux _____	c) carrying
4. nez _____	d) listening
5. oreilles _____	e) seeing
6. estomac _____	f) thinking
7. bouche _____	g) digesting
8. bras _____	h) writing
9. tête _____	i) touching
10. doigts _____	j) speaking

H Lis le passage. Choisis les réponses applicables.

Je m'appelle Jeanne-Marie. J'ai dix ans. Je suis fantastique! Avec la tête, je choisis les réponses applicables. Avec la bouche, je parle français. J'écris avec la main, et je marche avec les jambes. Avec les yeux, j'admire les peintures de Manet. Comme je suis fantastique!

1. Jeanne-Marie est. . . .
   a) un homme
   b) une fille
   c) un garçon
   d) une femme

2. Jeanne-Marie a . . . ans.
   a) onze
   b) dix-sept
   c) treize
   d) dix

3. Jeanne-Marie parle avec. . . .
   a) les mains
   b) les jambes
   c) la bouche
   d) les yeux

4. Avec les jambes, Jeanne-Marie. . . .
   a) marche
   b) écrit
   c) admire les peintures de Manet
   d) parle français

5. Comme Jeanne-Marie est . . . !
   a) jolie
   b) fantastique
   c) bonne
   d) belle

Les **yeux** de braise

Quels regards ! A en fondre. Ces six paires d'yeux appartiennent à des vedettes de tous les horizons. Qui sont-elles ?

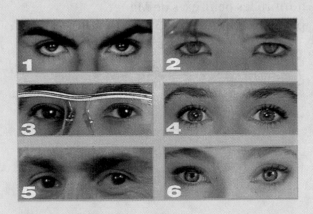

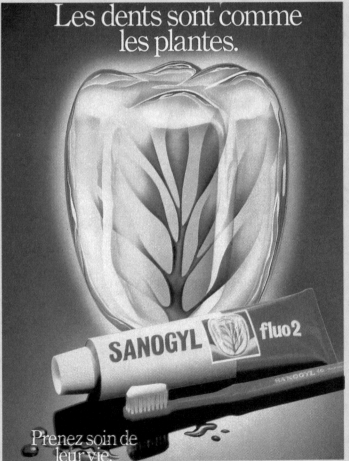

CLOTHING
Les Vêtements

Que portes-tu?
Je porte mes nouveaux vêtements.

What are you wearing?
I'm wearing my new clothes.

Evelyne
Vacances d'hiver
la Suisse—janvier

2 robes de laine
3 chapeaux
3 pyjamas
2 ceintures
3 mouchoirs
2 chandails
chaussettes
gants
pantalon
chaussures

2 chemisiers
manteau

Evelyne
Winter Vacation
Switzerland—January

2 woolen dresses
3 hats
3 pairs of pajamas
2 belts
3 handkerchiefs
2 woolen sweaters
socks
gloves
pants
shoes

2 blouses
overcoat

La mode par Suzanne
vêtements d'intérieur et de ville

chemisier

robe

cravate

blouson

robe de
chambre

jupe

pantoufles

chemise

costume

L'habit ne fait pas le moine.

You can't tell a book by its cover.

Exercises

A Match column B with column A.

A	**B**
1. jupe _____	a) handkerchief
2. vêtements de ville _____	b) jacket
3. pantalon _____	c) coat
4. cravate _____	d) necktie
5. gants _____	e) skirt
6. mouchoir _____	f) outer clothing
7. chandail _____	g) trousers
8. manteau _____	h) shoes
9. chaussures _____	i) gloves
10. blouson _____	j) sweater

B Que portes-tu...? (En français, s'il te plaît.)

1. to school _____

2. to a symphony concert _____

3. to bed _____

4. in cool weather _____

5. in cold weather _____

C Complete the analogies.

1. gants : mains = _____ : pieds

2. _____ : jupe = chemise : pantalon

3. robe de chambre : pyjama = manteau : _____

4. cravate : chemise = _____ : pantalon

D Complète chaque phrase selon l'illustration.

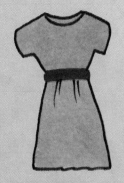

1. Je porte une _____.

2. Je porte un _____.

3. Je porte une _____.

4. Je porte une _____ et
   un _____ .

5. Je porte une _____
   et une _____.

E Écris les mots en anglais.

1. porter _____

2. il / elle porte _____

3. je porte _____

4. tu portes _____

F Complète en anglais.

1. A "chapeau" is worn on the _____.

2. A "ceinture" is worn around one's _____.

3. One wears a "pyjama" to _____.

4. A "jupe" is usually worn with a _____.

5. A "chaussure" is worn on a _____.

G List the required number of items for each category. (En français, s'il te plaît.)

outerwear (5)   **accessories (3)**

_____   _____

_____   _____

_____   _____

_____

_____

footwear (3)   **sleepwear (1)**

_____   _____

_____

_____

H Lis le passage. Choisis les réponses applicables.

Ce soir tu vas à l'opéra. Tes parents vont avec toi. Tu portes une robe très élégante. Parce qu'il fait froid, tu portes des gants et un manteau.

1. Qui va à l'opéra?
   a) tes parents et toi
   b) toute la classe
   c) ce soir

2. Que portes-tu?
   a) l'opéra
   b) une robe
   c) parents

3. Comment est la robe?
   a) belle
   b) grande
   c) élégante

4. Que portes-tu avec ton manteau?
   a) un chapeau
   b) une jupe
   c) des gants

Mots croisés

Vertical

1. Pair of slacks.
2. Handled with kid "...."
3. Sometimes dropped to begin a duel.
4. What a suitor wears on a date.
7. « L' . . . ne fait pas le moine. »

Horizontal

1. Customary sleepwear.
3. Worn in cold weather.
4. A fool talks through his " . . . . "
5. « Je . . . un chemisier. »
6. ". . . de chambre."
8. Neck garment.
9. Often worn with a blouse.
10. All things worn to keep in good health.

MICHEL KLEIN

375ᶠ

69ᶠ

H 129ᶠ H 129ᶠ H 225ᶠ

A 750ᶠ B 750ᶠ C 1150ᶠ

E 490ᶠ F 375ᶠ G 390ᶠ

I 375ᶠ

Le tee-shirt
22ᶠ

TEE-SHIRT
COL MONTANT
Manches longues.
100% coton.
Noir ou écru.
De la taille 2 à 5.

La chemise
60ᶠ

CHEMISE COMPLICES
55% ramie - 45% coton.
Col souple. Poches
poitrine. Bleu à carreaux.
Du 37/38
au 43/44.

Le jean's
57ᶠ

JEAN'S
100% coton.
Stone washed.
Du 36 au 48.

DERBY
Dessus croûte de cuir
velours de vachette.
Semelle élastomère.
Noir, marron ou
bordeaux. Du 39 au 45.

Les derby
56ᶠ

Les 4 articles
195ᶠ

149ᶠ

les gants 129 F

99ᶠ

69 F

89 F

TIME
AND COLORS
L'Heure et les Couleurs

Quelle heure est-il?
À quelle heure… ?

What time is it?
At what time…?

Il est une heure et demie.

Il est dix heures
moins le quart.

Il est trois heures.

Il est midi.

Il est sept heures
et quart.

Il est minuit.

Il est deux heures cinq.

Il est midi moins cinq.

 Transportation in Europe operates on official
time, which is on a twenty-four hour basis. Official
time is often used by schools, radio and television
stations, theaters and movie theaters.

 Mieux vaut tard que jamais.   Better late than never.

De quelle couleur est…?
Il
Elle } est…

De quelle couleur sont…?
Ils
Elles } sont…

What color is …?
It is…

What color are …?
They are…

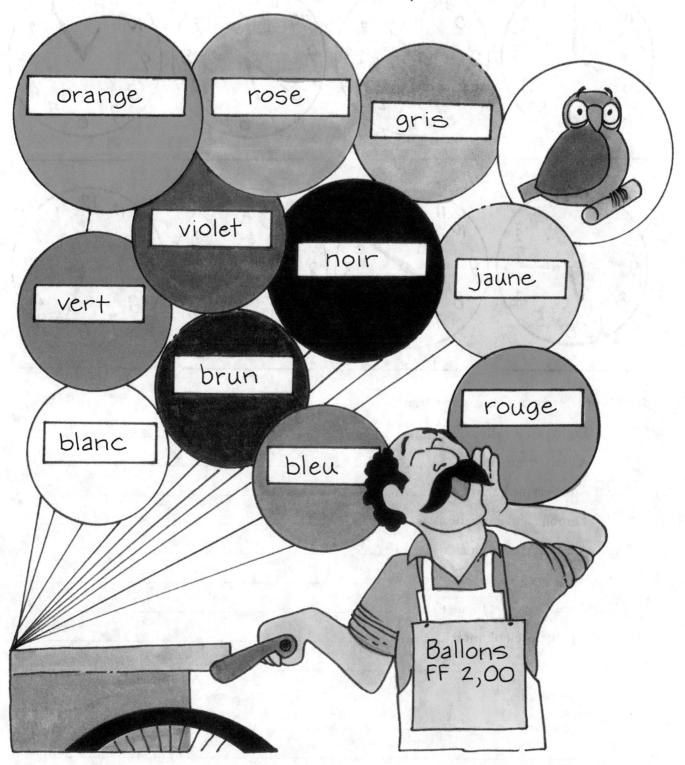

orange

rose

gris

violet

noir

jaune

vert

brun

rouge

blanc

bleu

Ballons
FF 2,00

A Listen as your teacher indicates a time. Find the clock that shows that time and label it number 1. Then your teacher will express another time. Mark the clock expressing that time number 2. Continue until all clocks are numbered.

_____ _____ _____ _____

_____ _____ _____ _____

B Complète chaque phrase en français.

1. Light red is called _____.

2. A "forget-me-not" is _____.

3. An overripe banana is _____.

4. Lemons and dandelions are _____.

5. A leaf in the summer is _____.

6. A chimney sweep is covered with _____ soot.

7. A fruit gives its name to this color: _____.

8. A healthy elephant is _____.

9. A _____ elephant is always found at this

   type of sale.

10. "_____ in the morning, sailors take warning.

    _____ at night, sailors' delight."

C   Écris en français.

1.   At seven o'clock. _____ .

2.   It's half past one. _____ .

3.   At 7:10. _____ .

4.   It's 2:40. _____ .

5.   At twenty after three. _____ .

D   De quelle couleur sont-ils?

A	B
1. Hearts and tomatoes _____	a) jaunes
2. Frogs and grass _____	b) gris
3. Lemons and corn _____	c) bleus
4. Elephants and rain clouds _____	d) rouges
5. Forget-me-nots and robins' eggs _____	e) vertes

E   Lis le passage. Choisis les réponses applicables.

Danielle va[1] au bal avec son ami Bernard. Ils aiment[2] danser. Ils aiment la musique classique et moderne. Danielle porte une robe blanche et rouge. Le costume de Bernard est bleu. Le bal commence à 19 h et finit à 22 h 30.

1.   Comment s'appelle la jeune fille?
     a) Bernard   b) Danielle

2.   Comment s'appelle le garçon?
     a) Bernard   b) Danielle

3.   Où vont Danielle et Bernard?
     a) au bal   b) au concert
     c) au cinéma   d) au jardin

4.   Quelle est la couleur du costume de Bernard?
     a) gris   b) blanc
     c) bleu   d) rouge

5.   À quelle heure finit le bal?
     a) à 18 h 30   b) à 19 h 30
     c) à 20 h 30   d) à 22 h 30

[1]**va** = is going   [2]**aiment** = like

Il est 8h.

Color the clock according to the directions.

1. Color the "nez" ROUGE.
2. Color the "yeux" BLEU.
3. Color the "cheveux" VERT.
4. Color the "figure" ORANGE.
5. Color the "bouche" ROSE.
6. Color the "pieds" NOIR.

7. Color the "quatre" GRIS.
8. Color the "six" VIOLET.
9. Color the "trois" ROUGE.
10. Color the *I* BLANC.
11. Color the *h* BRUN.
12. Color the *s* JAUNE.

AGFA MULTICONTRAST PREMIUM
TOUS LES BLANCS, TOUS LES NOIRS

PROVISION DE COULEURS

Filet traditionnel en passementerie
Bordures et poignées souples renforcées. 100 % coton. bleu
858.3552   jaune 858.3218
rouge 858.3560
25 F

habitat BASICS

HORLOGE

110F

Horloge en ABS. Mouvement à quartz. Garantie 2 ans. Vendue sans pile.
451614 blanche 451630 rouge
451657 aqua 456616 jaune
451649 gris metal

110 F

CROIX VERTE INTERNATIONALE
fondation à buts écologiques pour la protection de la terre.

CHAUMET
JOAILLIER DEPUIS 1780
PARIS

Une montre
peut se passer d'aiguilles.
La preuve par Chaumet.

12, PLACE VENDÔME - PARIS - (1) 44 77 24 00

MUSIC
La Musique

Three Great Musicians

Jean-Philippe Rameau (1683–1764) was born in Dijon. He was a superb musician who performed flawlessly on both the organ and the harpsichord. Rameau was also a great musical theorist whose works on harmony are still considered gems today. Rameau moved to Paris in 1732. There he composed church music, operas, ballets, and music for the harpsichord. Rameau tried to make French music truly French. Before his death he was recognized as the outstanding French composer of the Baroque Era. *Castor and Pollux* and *Pieces for the Harpsichord* are two of his noted works.

Georges Bizet (1838–75) was born in Paris, where his musical career began at the age of six. He entered the Paris Conservatory of Music at nine. At nineteen he won the Prix de Rome award. Bizet's opera *Carmen* is considered the best opera ever written by a French composer. It is exciting, dramatic, and colorful. The lack of immediate recognition of this work in his country caused Bizet sorrow and illness. He died at thirty-seven.

Maurice Ravel (1875–1937) was born in Ciboure. Like many of the composers of his time, Ravel used the folk music of France and its neighboring countries as the basis for his musical masterpieces. He used the large orchestra effectively to give life and color to his music. Ravel used different sounds to create different impressions. This is called impressionism. Besides his operas, ballets, and orchestral pieces, this brilliant composer wrote chamber music, piano works, and vocal pieces. Ravel died in Paris in 1937. *The Spanish Hour*, *Daphnis and Chloé*, and *The Waltz* are three of his works.

 C'est le ton qui fait la chanson. It's the manner that shows the intent.

Exercises

A Give the full name of the composer who:

1. used the large orchestra to enliven his music. _____

2. tried to make French music really French. _____

3. wrote a very famous opera. _____

B Match column B with column A.

A	**B**
1. *Carmen* _____	a) work by Ravel
2. *Castor and Pollux* _____	b) died disappointed
3. *The Waltz* _____	c) work by Rameau
4. Rameau _____	d) opera by Bizet
5. Bizet _____	e) great musical theorist

C Complete the analogies.

1. *The Waltz* : _____ = *Castor and Pollux* : Rameau

2. _____ : Bizet = *The Spanish Hour* : Ravel

3. Georges : _____ = Maurice : Ravel

4. church music : _____ = opera : Bizet

5. Dijon : Rameau = _____ : Ravel

D Answer the following questions correctly.

1. Who wrote the best French opera? _____

2. What was one of Rameau's favorite instruments? _____

3. What was the name of the award that Bizet won? _____

4. What is a musical work of Rameau? _____

5. Who tried to keep French music truly French? _____

E Écris les noms correctement.

1. ROGEEGS _____

2. CAUMEIR _____

3. TIZBE _____

4. LARVE _____

5. MAUEAR _____

F Match the name with the illustration.

Bizet

Ravel

Rameau

G

Vertical

2. Best French opera.
4. Utilized entirely by Ravel.
8. Birthplace of Rameau.

Horizontal

1. First name of impressionist composer.
3. Rameau wrote books about . . . .
5. Birthplace of Ravel.
6. First part of first name of Baroque composer.
7. Composer of *Carmen*.
9. Birthplace of Bizet.
10. The Prix de . . . was awarded to Bizet.

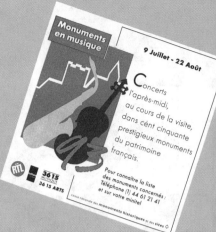

15

WEATHER AND SEASONS
Le Temps et les Saisons

Quel temps fait-il?

Il fait beau.

Comme ci, comme ça.

How's the weather?

Il fait mauvais.

Il fait du soleil.	It's sunny.	Il fait frais.	It's cool.
Il fait chaud.	It's warm (hot).	Il fait du vent.	It's windy.
		Il fait humide.	It's humid.
		Le temps est couvert.	It's overcast.

Il fait froid.	It's cold.
Il y a des éclairs.	It's lightning.
Il neige.	It's snowing.
Il y a du tonnerre.	It's thundering.
Il pleut.	It's raining.

Quelle est la saison?
C'est...

What's the season?
It's ....

Les quatre saisons

le printemps

l'automne

l'hiver

l'été

Use "au" before "printemps" and "en" before the other seasons to express English "in" + season(s).

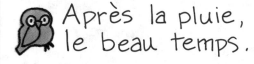 Après la pluie,
le beau temps.

Every cloud has a
silver lining.

Exercises

A   Match the sentence with the illustration.

1. _____ a) Il fait du soleil.

2. _____ b) Il y a des éclairs.

3. _____ c) Il pleut.

4. _____ d) Il fait du vent.

5. _____ e) Il fait froid.

98

B Quel temps fait-il? Réponds à la question en français.

1. _____

2. _____

3. _____

4. _____

5. _____

C   **Match the season with the illustration.**

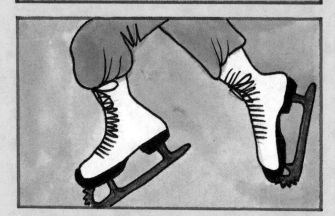

1. _____ a) été

2. _____ b) hiver

3. _____ c) printemps

4. _____ d) automne

D Match the verbs with the nouns.

A	**B**
(Nouns)	*(Verbs)*
1. pluie _____	a) neiger
2. neige _____	b) avoir des éclairs
3. tonnerre _____	c) faire du soleil
4. éclair _____	d) pleuvoir
5. soleil _____	e) avoir du tonnerre

E Write in **Column 1** the English meaning of the words at the left. When you have finished the entire column, cover the column of words at the left, and in **Column 2** change the English words into French.

		Column 1	**Column 2**
		(English)	*(French)*
1.	soleil	_____	_____
2.	éclairs	_____	_____
3.	printemps	_____	_____
4.	été	_____	_____
5.	temps	_____	_____
6.	automne	_____	_____
7.	saison	_____	_____
8.	frais	_____	_____
9.	chaud	_____	_____
10.	Il pleut.	_____	_____
11.	hiver	_____	_____
12.	mauvais	_____	_____
13.	tonnerre	_____	_____
14.	froid	_____	_____

F Quel temps fait-il? *Using the cue at the left, write a statement about the weather.* (En français, s'il te plaît.)

1. (Rain, wind, and hail) _____.

2. (Outdoor tennis court) _____.

3. (Sailboat) _____.

4. (Cardigan sweater) _____.

5. (Air conditioner) _____.

6. (Lightning bolts) _____.

7. (Snowflakes) _____.

8. (Sunglasses) _____.

9. (Umbrella) _____.

10. (Mittens and parka) _____.

G Lis le passage. Choisis les réponses applicables.

Les Quatre Saisons

En hiver, il fait très froid. Tout le monde fait du ski. Au printemps, il fait frais et il pleut beaucoup. Il fait chaud en été et il fait du soleil. En automne, il fait du vent et il fait frais aussi. Les quatre saisons sont fantastiques.

1. En hiver . . .
    a) il fait mauvais   c) il fait froid
    b) il y a du tonnerre   d) il fait chaud

2. Il pleut beaucoup . . .
    a) en hiver   c) au printemps
    b) en éte   d) en automne

3. En été . . .
    a) il fait beau   c) il y a des éclairs
    b) il fait frais   d) il neige

4. L'automne est une . . .
    a) pluie   c) couleur
    b) neige   d) saison

Mots croisés

H

Vertical

1. Sunbathing can be dangerous when it's "...."
3. Opposite of "beau."
4. « Il fait ... »
6. Celestial explosions.
7. Accompany thunder.
10. Somewhat "froid."
12. Opposite of summer.
13. Needed to fly kites.
14. "Il ..." cats and dogs.

Horizontal

2. « Les quatre... »
5. The "..." is the baseball season.
8. Halloween occurs in "...."
9. Opposite of "froid."
11. Much colder than "frais."
14. Season of new growth.
15. Light of the day.
16. « Quel... fait-il? »

DAYS AND MONTHS
Les Jours et les Mois

Quel jour est-ce?
C'est...

What day is today?
Today is....

Monday lundi	mardi	mercredi	jeudi	vendredi	samedi	dimanche
	1	2	3	4	5	6
7	8	9	10	11	12	13
14	15	16	17	18	19	20
21	22	23	24	25	26	27
28	29	30	31			

Quelle est la date aujourd'hui?
C'est le premier mai.
le quatorze juillet.
le vingt-cinq novembre.
26 - 4 - 95.

What is the date today?
It's May first.
July 14.
November 25.
4-26-95.

avril
mai
juin

octobre
novembre
décembre

janvier
février
mars

juillet
août
septembre

 Ne remettez pas au lendemain
ce que vous pouvez faire aujourd'hui.

Never put off until tomorrow
what you can do today.

Cahier de Jacques

Apprends pour l'examen d'anglais:

1. tomorrow (mon anniversaire)
2. the day after tomorrow
3. yesterday
4. the day before yesterday
5. the day
6. the holiday; party (bravo!)
7. the school day
8. the birthday   (demain)
9. the week
10. the weekend   (ma vie!)
11. the month

Jacque's notebook

Learn for English Test:

1. demain
2. après-demain
3. hier
4. avant-hier
5. le jour
6. la fête
7. le jour de classe
8. l'anniversaire
9. la semaine
10. la fin de semaine, le week-end
11. le mois

Weekdays and Mythology

Derivations and Comparisons

French Day	Roman Mythology
Lundi	Day honoring the moon god. *Luna* = "moon."
Mardi	Day honoring Mars, god of war.
Mercredi	Day honoring Mercury, messenger of the gods.
Jeudi	Day honoring Jupiter, or Jove, father of the gods.
Vendredi	Day honoring Venus, goddess of love.
Samedi	Day honoring Saturn, god of the harvest and agriculture.
Dimanche	Day honoring the Lord. *Dominus* = "the Lord." Christian conversion of *solis dies* = "day of the sun."

Exercises

A Write in numerical form the dates that your teacher reads.

1. _____

2. _____

3. _____

4. _____

5. _____

B Label the current month. Include the names of the days and all the numbers.

MOIS _____

JOUR	JOUR	JOUR	JOUR	JOUR	JOUR	JOUR

C Écris les dates.

1. Monday, July 14th. _____

2. Saturday, July 25th. _____

3. Tuesday, January 1st. _____

4. Wednesday, November 11th. _____

5. Sunday, August 15th. _____

D Match column B with column A.

A	B
1. aujourd'hui _____	a) yesterday
2. après-demain _____	b) day after tomorrow
3. avant-hier _____	c) today
4. demain _____	d) tomorrow
5. hier _____	e) day before yesterday

E Écris en français.

1. The third month of the year. _____

2. The "mois" in which school ends. _____

3. The second "jour" of the school week. _____

4. The month that "brings May flowers." _____

5. The first day of the week. _____

6. The month of the French national holiday. _____

7. An autumn month of thirty days. _____

8. The last day of the "semaine." _____

9. The day that precedes Tuesday. _____

10. The month in which Halloween is celebrated. _____

F Écris le nom du jour selon l'illustration.

1. _____

2. _____

3. _____

4. _____

5.

6.

7. _____

G Lis le passage. Choisis les réponses applicables.

C'est aujourd'hui mercredi et Françoise est heureuse. Le Tour de France arrive dans sa ville. C'est une course de bicyclette dans toute la France. Françoise a une bonne place pour regarder la course. Demain elle va à une fête pour enfants. Ce week-end elle va jouer au football. La semaine de Françoise est une bonne semaine.

1. Qui est heureuse?
   a) la France   b) une bicyclette
   c) la ville   d) Françoise

2. Le Tour de France est une bonne place, n'est-ce pas?
   a) oui   b) non

3. Où est cette course?
   a) en ville   b) à la fête
   c) dans toute la France   d) au football

4. Quand est la fête?
   a) mercredi   b) mardi
   c) samedi   d) jeudi

5. Est-ce que Françoise reste à la maison ce week-end?
   a) oui   b) non

Mots croisés

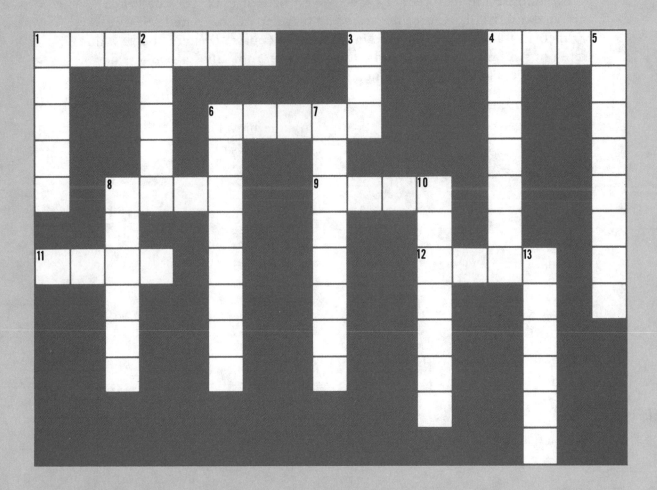

H

Vertical

1. Day before "vendredi."
2. Day that begins the week.
3. Floral month.
4. Resolution month.
5. Thanksgiving month.
6. Mercury is honored on " . . . . "
7. Last or first day of the week.
8. A day has twenty-four of these.
10. "Sept jours."
13. Saturday.

Horizontal

1. Warmest summer month.
4. Month in which summer begins.
6. Day named for Mars.
8. The day just past.
9. A thirty-day period.
11. One seventh of a week.
12. The god and the month have the same name.

T F 1

LUNDI
20.40 FILM TV
NAVARRO
FILS DE PERIPH'
de Denys Granier-Deferre
avec Roger Hanin

22.35 FILM
LA BONNE ANNEE
de Claude Lelouch

MARDI
20.45 FILM
**TAIS-TOI
QUAND TU PARLES**
de Philippe Clair
avec Aldo Maccione,
Edwige Fenech

22.25 FILM
LE RETOUR DE SABATA
de Frank Kramer

MERCREDI
20.45 FILM TV
**TAILLE
MANNEQUIN**
de Henri Safran
avec Heather Thomas,
Andrew Clarke

22.55 MAGAZINE
52 SUR LA UNE
AMOURS DE FEMMES

JEUDI
20.45 FEUILLETON
**LES OISEAUX
SE CACHENT
POUR MOURIR**
avec Richard Chamberlain

22.25 SERIE
LES DESSOUS DE PALM BEACH
DUEL DE FEMMES

VENDREDI
20.45 FEUILLETON
**LES GRANDES
MAREES**
de Jean Sagols
avec Nicole Calfan,
Bernard Le Coq

22.25 DIVERTISSEMENT
COUCOU C'EST NOUS
LES MEILLEURS MOMENTS

SAMEDI
20.45 DIVERTISSEMENT
SUCCES FOUS

22.50 FILM

20.45

DIMANCHE

GÉMEAUX
22 mai
21 juin

LE VRAI
BONHEUR

TAUREAU
21 avril
21 mai

TENDRESSE
ET CARESSES

CANCER
22 juin
22 juillet

OUVRE
LES YEUX

LION
23 juillet
23 août

LAISSE
TOMBER !

BALANCE
24 septembre
23 octobre

JOIE
DE VIVRE

VERSEAU
21 janvier
18 février

TRÈS
BRILLANTE

POISSONS
19 février
20 mars

TROP
EXIGEANTE

LES PLUS BEAUX CONCERTS

- 28 avril NEIL YOUNG
- 3 mai DURAN DURAN
- 4 mai ALAIN CHAMFORT
- 7 mai SANTANA
- 26 mai TINA TURNER
- 30 mai JANE BIRKIN

AVEC

NRJ

94.5

ZENITH

17

LITERATURE
La Littérature

Three Great Authors

Pierre Corneille (1606–84) was born in Rouen. He studied the classics, Latin and Greek, and excelled in them. Following family tradition, he studied law and practiced in Rouen. Because of a speech impediment, he decided to abandon law and to write plays. He moved to Paris and published his first drama, *Mélite*. The play was a success and launched Corneille on a very successful career. Corneille wrote many great plays based on the exploits of Greek and Roman heroes. However, his masterpiece, *Le Cid*, is a play that uses a national hero of Spain as its principal character. Corneille is considered today the father of French classical drama.

Victor Hugo (1802-85) was a sensitive writer who was sincerely interested in literature, politics, and his fellow man. His novels speak of concern for the less fortunate and the handicapped, who were often the innocent victims of unjust laws. His efforts on behalf of thses poor people caused him to be sent into exile by his government. Hugo was a superb novelist and an excellent poet and dramatist. Many think that he is the best writer of the romantic period in France. Some of his works are *Hernani, Les Misérables*, and *Les Feuilles d'automne* (*The Autumn Leaves*).

Charles Baudelaire (1821–67) was born in Paris. He was intelligent and liked poetry and art greatly. His mother and stepfather tried to force him to follow a more profitable career. Baudelaire decided to follow his own star and began his writing career. He was not immediately successful and was forced to write art essays to earn his food. Baudelaire loved languages and read the German poets. E.T.A. Hoffmann was his favorite. Baudelaire even translated the poems of Edgar Allan Poe into French. Baudelaire tried to explain life and its events with word pictures or symbols. A pretty flower could be a sign of joy or good, while a wilting flower could be a sign of sorrow or evil. This is called symbolism. Baudelaire was a master of this type of poetry. He wrote a collection of poems, called *Les Fleurs du mal*, that brought him fame. Tortured by poverty and ill health, Baudelaire died at the age of forty-six.

Tout est bien qui finit bien.   All's well that ends well.

Exercises

A   Guess who...

1. abandoned law to write plays. _____

2. revealed the suffering of the poor and unfortunate. _____

3. studied and mastered Greek and Latin. _____

4. was discouraged from pursuing a career as a poet. _____

5. enjoyed the stories of E.T.A. Hoffmann. _____

B   Match column B with column A.

A	**B**
1. Pierre Corneille _____	a) novel of social injustice
2. Victor Hugo _____	b) great poet and art critic
3. Charles Baudelaire _____	c) Corneille's greatest play
4. *Le Cid* _____	d) famous romantic author
5. *Les Misérables* _____	e) father of French classical drama

C   Write the full name of the author of each work listed below.

1. *Mélite*: _____

2. *Hernani*: _____

3. *Les Fleurs du mal*: _____

4. *Les Misérables*: _____

5. *Le Cid*: _____

D   Complete the analogies.

1. Roman heroes : classicism = the downtrodden : _____

2. _____ : Baudelaire = drama : Corneille

3. novel : _____ = poem : Baudelaire

4. Rouen : Corneille = Paris : _____

5. art : Baudelaire = _____ : Corneille

E   Groupe le nom avec l'illustration.

Baudelaire

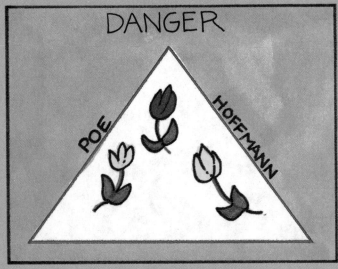

Hugo

Corneille

F Which author would most likely...

1. enjoy David's painting, *The Death of Socrates*?

   _____

2. write a letter to a newspaper protesting the government's abuse of a poor beggar?

   _____

3. describe moods in terms of colors?

   _____

4. have benefited by government aid to poets?

   _____

G Label each plot described below as modern, romantic, or classical.

1. Professor Horatio Allgood has the opportunity to be appointed Commissioner of Education for the republic of Scholarium. To receive this honor he must agree to be silent about a national committee that has unjustly fired a fellow professor. Professor Allgood does his duty and speaks out. His courageous action clears his colleague's name, but Professor Allgood loses the appointment. _____

2. Jean-Pierre L'Amour is devastated over the loss of his girlfriend, Gigi. He joins the French Foreign Legion and dies heroically. In his hand is found a picture of Gigi.

   _____

3. In the poem "Pulsating Pineapple" the star-shaped potato is about to take a trip on the jet stream to see the fawn-colored fragrance about conducting business with the maroon meloncrests. _____

H Complète les phrases.

1. _____ displeased his parents by becoming a poet.

2. _____ studied law in Paris.

3. _____ was a great writer of the romantic period.

4. _____ was a great classical dramatist.

5. _____ translated the writings of Edgar Allan Poe into French.

6. _____ told of the suffering of the poor and the handicapped.

7. _____ was sent into exile by his government.

8. _____ abandoned a law career to write plays.

9. _____ was a famous symbolist poet.

10. _____ wrote world-famous novels.

Nouveautés
Roman Jeunesse

Bertrand Gauthier
LA REVANCHE D'ANI CROCHE

la courte échelle — Roman Jeunesse

13. La revanche
d'Ani Croche
texte: Bertrand Gauthier
illustrations: Gérard Frischeteau

14. La montagne Noire
texte: Chrystine Brouillet
illustrations: Philippe Brochard

15. Le mystère du lac Carré
texte: Sylvie Desrosiers
illustrations: Daniel Sylvestre

16. Le roi de rien
texte: Raymond Plante
illustrations: Jules Prud'homme

la courte échelle

ROBIN WILLIAMS

Il fut leur inspiration. Il a transformé leur vie à jamais.

LE CERCLE DES POETES DISPARUS

UN FILM DE PETER WEIR

TOUCHSTONE PICTURES ... SILVER SCREEN PARTNERS IV ... STEVEN HAFT
WITT-THOMAS PRODUCTIONS ... PETER WEIR ROBIN WILLIAMS "LE CERCLE DES POETES DIS
(DEAD POETS SOCIETY) ... MAURICE JARRE ... JOHN SEALE, A.C.S. ... TOM SCHULMAN
... STEVEN HAFT PAUL JUNGER WITT TONY THOMAS ... PETER WEIR

**MON AMOUR
(pour Christophe)**
Valérie, Heuringhem

C'est pour toi,
Oui, c'est pour toi,
Pour toi ces phrases.
Ça ne veut rien dire,
Mais pour moi,
Cela vient au fond de moi,
Du fond de mon cœur,
De mon amour éternel.
Un jour, tu reviendras,
Je le sais bien,
Car tu m'aimes encore
Et moi plus encore.
Je te promets
Que, le jour où nous
ressortirons ensemble,
Je te ferai lire ce poème,
Car il t'est destiné.
Et moi je t'offrirai
Mon amour.

MICHAEL CRICHTON

LE PARC JURASSIQUE
ROMAN
ROBERT LAFFONT

LE PARC JURASSIQUE.
Michael Crichton .
Roman de science-fiction.
Une découverte scientifique
majeure qui tourne à la
catastrophe. Nul ne peut
dominer la Nature. Bientôt
porté à l'écran par Spiel-
berg en personne.
114 F.

UN CLASSIQUE DE WALT DISNEY
Le Livre de la Jungle

THE PALACE THEATRE
Les Misérables

Nouveautés
Premier Roman

Marie-Francine Hébert
Un blouson dans la peau

la courte échelle — Premier Roman

5. Le blabla des jumeaux
texte: Bertrand Gauthier
illustrations: Daniel Dumont

6. Un blouson dans la peau
texte: Marie-Francine Hébert
illustrations: Philippe Germain

7. Babouche est jalouse
texte: Gilles Gauthier
illustrations: Pierre-André Derome

8. Véloville
texte: Raymond Plante
illustrations: Lise Monette

la courte échelle

18

LEISURE AND RECREATION
Les Loisirs et les Divertissements

Où vas-tu?

Where are you going?

Je vais au match.
I'm going to the game.

Je vais au musée.
I'm going to the museum.

Je vais à la boum.
I'm going to the party.

Je vais à la plage.
I'm going to the beach.

Raymond:	Où vas-tu ce soir?	Where are you going tonight?
Samuel:	Je vais au match.	I'm going to the game.
Raymond:	Moi aussi!	Me, too!

❀❀❀❀❀❀

André:	Où vas-tu aujourd'hui?	Where are you going today?
Brigitte:	Je vais au musée...au Louvre.*	I'm going to the museum...to the Louvre.
André:	Pourquoi?	Why?
Brigitte:	Pour voir le festival Delacroix.	To see the Delacroix Festival.

* The Louvre, France's most prominent art museum, is located in Paris.

Diversité réjouit.   Variety is the spice of life.

Je fais du volley-ball.
I play volleyball.

Je fais du football.
I play soccer.

Quels sports fais-tu?
What sports do you play?

Je fais du basket-ball.
I play basketball.

Je fais du tennis.
I play tennis.

Je fais du base-ball.
I play baseball.

Qu'est-ce que tu aimes faire?
What do you like to do?

J'aime faire du ski.
I like skiing.

J'aime faire du cheval.
I like horseback riding.

J'aime lire.
I like reading.

J'aime danser.
I like dancing.

J'aime nager.
I like swimming.

J'aime faire du vélo.
I like biking.

Valérie:	Demain il y a un pique-nique.	Tomorrow there's a picnic.
Julie:	Où ça?	Where's that?
Valérie:	À la plage. Tu veux m'accompagner?	At the beach. Do you want to go with me?
Julie:	Oui. J'adore nager.	Yes. I love swimming.

❀❀❀❀❀

Catherine:	Tu vas à la boum ce soir?	Are you going to the party tonight?
Jean:	Bien sûr. Il y a de la musique, n'est-ce pas?	Of course. There'll be music, won't there?
Catherine:	Oui. J'adore danser.	Yes. I love dancing.

A Où vas-tu? Complète chaque phrase en français.

1. Je vais au _____ . *(game)*

2. Je vais à la _____ . *(party)*

3. Je vais au _____ . *(museum)*

4. Je vais à la _____ . *(beach)*

B Select the correct answers based on the previous dialogues.

1. C'est quand le match?
    a) demain   b) vendredi
    c) ce soir   d) à 8 heures

2. Qu'est-ce que c'est que le Louvre?
    a) un cheval   b) un match
    c) le festival Delacroix   d) un musée

3. Delacroix, qui est-ce?
    a) un professeur   b) un artiste
    c) un musée   d) un acteur

4. C'est quand le pique-nique?
    a) demain   b) aujourd'hui
    c) à la plage   d) moi aussi

5. Où est le pique-nique?
    a) à la boum   b) au Louvre
    c) du base-ball   d) à la plage

C   Quels sports fais-tu? Complète chaque phrase en français.

1. Je fais _____ .

2. Je fais _____ .

3. Je fais _____ .

4. Je fais _____ .

5. Je fais _____ .

D Écris les mots correctement.

1. ctham _____

2. qneuiipeuq- _____

3. legap _____

4. mobu _____

5. emesu _____

E Qu'est-ce que tu aimes faire? Complète chaque phrase en français.

1. J'aime _____ .

2. J'aime _____ .

3. J'aime _____ .

4. J'aime _____ .

5. J'aime _____ .

6. J'aime _____ .

F Complète le dialogue en français.

Nadège: Où _____ -tu aujourd'hui?

Patrice: Je vais _____ la plage.

Tu _____ m'accompagner?

Nadège: Bien _____ . J'adore l'océan.

Patrice: Moi _____ ! Quels

_____ fais-tu à la plage?

Nadège: J'aime _____ dans l'océan et

je _____ du volley-ball.

G Lis le passage. Choisis les réponses applicables.

Céline organise une petite fête à la plage pour son anniversaire.[1] Aujourd'hui elle a douze ans. Elle invite ses amis Yvette, Hervé, Didier, Fabienne et Jean-Marcel à la fête. La fête commence à trois heures. Il fait chaud et la plage est très belle. Les amis aiment nager dans l'océan et faire du volley-ball. Après[2] les divertissements tout le monde a faim. Il y a un bon pique-nique avec des sandwichs, des boissons et de la glace. La fête d'anniversaire à la plage est magnifique!

1. Quel âge a Céline?
    a) treize ans   b) trois ans
    c) douze ans   d) onze ans

2. Qui va à la fête de Céline?
    a) ses parents   b) ses amis
    c) ses sœurs   d) tout le monde

3. Quel temps fait-il?
    a) Il fait beau.   b) Il pleut.
    c) Il neige.   d) Il fait froid.

4. Quel sport fait tout le monde?
    a) Tout le monde fait du ski.   b) Tout le monde a faim.
    c) Tout le monde fait du volley-ball. d) Tout le monde aime faire du cheval.

5. Qu'est-ce qu'il y a à manger?
    a) la plage   b) au restaurant
    c) des sandwichs   d) un volley-ball

[1] anniversaire=birthday   [2] Après=After

MAIRIE DE PARIS

DIRECTION DE LA JEUNESSE ET DES SPORTS

SERVICE DES SPORTS
25, BOULEVARD BOURDON - 75004 PARIS

N° 410835

TENNIS MUNICIPAUX
DEMI-HEURE PLEIN TARIF

TENNIS du
LUXEMBOURG

1re CATÉGORIE

INDIVIDUELS

ENTREE MUSEE

Réunion des musées nationaux

16F0 000451

LOUVRE

droit
d'entrée

SPÉCIAL ÉTÉ ABONNEMENTS
PROMOTIONNELS

- Piscine
- Squash   1 mois **250** F ttc
- Musculation
- Danse - Gym   3 mois **600** F ttc
- Rock'n Roll   sur présentation de ce chèque
- Sauna - Jaccusi

19, rue de Pontoise - 75005 PARIS
M° Maubert Mutualité - Tél. 43.54.82.45

CLUB
QUARTIER LATIN

UJA
ALFORTVILLE
RECRUTE
JEUNES FOOTBALLEURS

☐ né entre   ET   ☐ né entre
le 1/08/80   le 1/08/78
et 31/07/82   et 31/07/80

Ces jeunes footballeurs : ▶ ■ Bénéficieront d'un
encadrement nombreux et compétent
■ Pourront assister gratuitement à plusieurs matchs du
PSG accompagnés de leurs éducateurs
■ Partiront pour un tournoi au moins en fin de saison

TEL POUR RENSEIGNEMENTS

☎ — 43 75 61 35 —

Les Plages
de Cavalière

 FRANCE LOISIRS
LE CLUB OÙ IL FAIT BON LIRE

Lac Beauport
Sublime!
Une oasis de verdure et de
plein-air en toute saison.

À 15 minutes de Québec

Hébergement:
hébergement toutes
catégories, salle à
manger, brunch, bar,
piscine, congrès.

Auberge La Forêt Noire
(418) 849-7402

Auberge Les Quatres-
Temps (418) 849-4486

Manoir St-Castin
(418) 849-4461 ou
1-800-463-4824

Château Lac Beauport
(418) 849-2895

Le Saisonnier
(418) 849-2821

Activités plein air:
familles et groupes: golf,
voile, natation,
équitation, bicyclette,
promenade en carriole,
patinage, ski acrobatique.

Cité Joie
(équipement pour handicapés)
(418) 849-7183

Club Mont Tourbillon
(418) 849-4418

Centre de ski:
ski alpin, ski de fond,
jour et soir, école de ski,
location.

Le Relais
(418) 849-3073

Mont St-Castin
(418) 849-6776

Association Touristique de Lac Beauport Box 1101, Lac Beauport, Québec, Canada, G0A 2C0

19

SHOPPING
Les Achats

Je fais mes achats...
I shop...

le vendeur
salesclerk

la cliente
customer

les baskets (m.)
athletic shoes

...au centre commercial.
...at the shopping center (mall).

Anne:	Où vas-tu?	Where are you going?
Frédéric:	Au centre commercial.	To the shopping center.
Anne:	Qu'est-ce que tu vas acheter?	What are you going to buy?
Frédéric:	Des baskets.	Some athletic shoes.

❀❀❀❀❀

Vendeur:	Bonjour, Madame. Est-ce que je peux vous aider?	Hello, Ma'am. May I help you?
Cliente:	Non, merci. Je regarde seulement.	No thanks. I'm just looking.

 Premier arrivé, premier servi. First come, first served.

Client: Ce CD, c'est combien?	How much is this CD?
Caissière: Ça coûte 75,00 francs.	It costs 75 francs.
Client: C'est un peu cher!	That's a little expensive!
Caissière: Mais non, c'est bon marché.	No, it's cheap.
Client: Bon, je l'achète. Voilà, Mademoiselle.	OK, I'll buy it. There you are, Miss.
Caissière: Merci beaucoup. Voilà la monnaie.	Thank you very much. Here's your change.

Vendeuse: Quelque chose d'autre?	Anything else?
Client: Euh...trois tomates, cinq pêches et des haricots verts. Oui, c'est tout.	Uhm...three tomatoes, five peaches and some green beans. Yes, that's all.

Exercises

A Match the name of the store in column B with what you can buy there in column A.

	A			B	
	A			**B**	
1.	baskets	_____	a)	market
2.	haricots verts	_____	b)	shoe store
3.	CD	_____	c)	furniture store
4.	chaise	_____	d)	stationery store
5.	stylos et cahiers	_____	e)	music store

B Complète chaque phrase selon l'illustration.

1. J'adore les _____ .

2. Madame Blanchard choisit de beaux fruits au

_____ .

3. Je fais mes achats au

   _____ .

4. Voilà la _____ ,

   Monsieur.

5. Le CD est bon marché. Il

   _____

   50,00 francs.

C Choose the expression from the following list that completes each sentence correctly.

bon marché   francs   acheter

caisse   achats

Alix fait ses _____ au magasin. Elle va

_____ un CD de musique classique. Voilà un bon CD

à 55,00 _____ . Ce n'est pas cher. C'est

_____ . Elle va à la

_____ avec son CD.

D Réponds aux questions.

1. If you see the sign "Soldes," how would you expect the price of the object to be?
   a) bon marché   b) l'argent
   c) cher   d) la monnaie

2. What do you reply if the cashier says "Ça coûte 100,00 francs"?
   a) Voilà l'argent.   b) Où est le magasin?
   c) C'est combien?   d) Merci, c'est tout.

3. What do you get back if you give the cashier too much money?
   a) la caisse   b) la monnaie
   c) bon marché   d) des haricots verts

4. Who helps you find what you need?
   a) l'argent   b) le vendeur
   c) la caissière   d) la cliente

5. What do you say if you don't need the salesclerk's help right now?
   a) Est-ce que je peux vous aider?   b) C'est un peu cher!
   c) Je regarde seulement.   d) Quelque chose d'autre?

E Choisis la réponse correcte.

1. C'est tout?
   a) Non, je ne peux pas vous aider.
   b) Non...euh...des pêches, s'il vous plaît.
   c) Mais non, c'est bon marché.
   d) Non, je regarde seulement.

2. Pourquoi vas-tu au magasin?
   a) Je n'ai pas soif.
   b) Je porte une robe.
   c) Il y a un pique-nique.
   d) Je fais mes achats.

3. Les baskets, c'est bon marché?
   a) Oui, voilà la monnaie.
   b) Non, c'est le vendeur.
   c) Non, c'est cher.
   d) Oui, c'est tout.

4. Le CD, c'est combien?
   a) C'est 60,00 francs.
   b) Euh...je regarde seulement.
   c) C'est tout.
   d) Au centre commercial.

5. Qu'est-ce que tu vas acheter?
   a) soldes
   b) un vendeur
   c) des tomates et des haricots verts
   d) la monnaie

F Théo is shopping in a clothing store. Complete his conversation with the salesclerk.

Vendeur: Bonjour, Monsieur. Est-ce que je peux vous

_____ ?

Théo: Non, merci. Je _____ seulement.

Vendeur: C'est la saison des soldes. Tout est bon marché: les chemises, les

pantalons, les manteaux et les chaussures.

Théo: Merci, Monsieur. Euh...ce pantalon noir, c'est

_____ ?

Vendeur: Ca _____

200,00 _____ . C'est bon marché,

n'est-ce pas?

Théo: Mais non, c'est un peu _____ . Je ne peux

pas _____ le pantalon. J'ai

_____ 100,00 francs.

G

Vertical

2. What you pay your bill with.
3. «Non, merci. Je regarde....»
4. «Premier..., premier servi.»
5. «C'est...(*all*).»
6. «Est-ce que je peux vous...?»
7. Fruit that has a fuzzy exterior.
8. A female customer.
10. The opposite of "bon marché."
13. Compact disc.
14. «...vas-tu?»

Horizontal

1. Sporty "chaussures."
4. «Quelque chose d'...?»
9. A shopping center.
11. A cash register.
12. "Les...verts."
15. Where you buy fresh vegetables.
16. A female salesclerk.

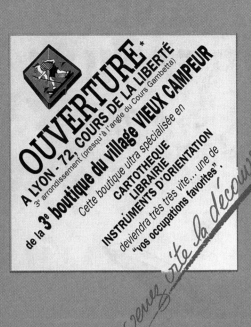

OUVERTURE*

A LYON - 72, COURS DE LA LIBERTÉ
3e arrondissement (presqu'à l'angle du Cours Gambetta)
de la 3e boutique du village VIEUX CAMPEUR
Cette boutique ultra spécialisée en
CARTOTHÈQUE
LIBRAIRIE
INSTRUMENTS D'ORIENTATION
deviendra très très vite... une de
"vos occupations favorites".

venez vite la découvrir !

CARTES DE CRÉDIT
Nous acceptons les Cartes de Crédit =
AURORE/Cetelem, **PLURIEL**/Franfinance et
CARTE BLEUE/Sofinco.

Si vous n'avez pas encore de
Compte Permanent, nous procéderons
à l'ouverture de celui-ci.

*Un compact-disc, c'est inusable
un compact d'occasion, c'est quoi ?*

PRIX DISCOUNT TOUTE L'ANNÉE

GALERIES Lafayette

PRINTEMPS

Le Grand Magasin
Capitale de la Mode

GALERIES LAFAYETTE, 40, bd Haussmann - Tél. 42.82.36.40

C'est moins cher

FORUM DES HALLES
L'ARCHI-SHOPPING
DANS LES ARCHI-BOUTIQUES

260 BOUTIQUES

AU CENTRE DE PARIS

CENTRALE D'ACHAT
OPERA DISTRIBUTION
DISTRIBUTEUR DES PLUS
GRANDES MARQUES.

■

30, rue Cauchy - 75015 PARIS
De 10 h à 19 h du mardi au samedi

SOLDES
du 21 juin au 31 juillet
• TELE • HIFI • VIDEO
• ELECTRO-MENAGER • PHOTOS
• TELEPHONIE • AUTORADIO

Des prix à couper le souffle !
une visite s'impose...

*Le meilleur accueil et les meilleurs prix seront
réservés au porteur de ce bon TRANSFAC.*

20

TRAVEL AND TRANSPORTATION

Les Voyages et les Moyens de transport

Comment voyages-tu ?

How do you travel?

Je voyage en avion.
I travel by plane.

Je voyage en autobus.
I travel by bus.

Je voyage en voiture.
I travel by car.

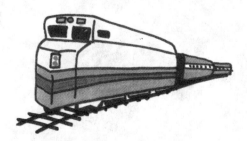

Je voyage en train.
I travel by train.

Je voyage en navire.
I travel by ship.

 On s'instruit en voyageant.   Whoever travels far knows much.

à l'aéroport
at the airport

l'employée (f.)
clerk

le passeport
passport

la valise
suitcase

le guichet
ticket counter

le voyageur
traveler

Employée:	Votre passeport, Monsieur?	Your passport, Sir?
Voyageur:	C'est dans ma valise, Mademoiselle.	It's in my suitcase, Miss.
Employée:	Mais il faut l'avoir sur vous...et surtout au contrôle des passeports en arrivant.	But you must have it on you...and especially at passport control upon arrival.
Voyageur:	D'accord. Attendez.... Et on monte où?	OK. Wait.... And where do we board?
Employée:	À la porte 20, à droite.	At gate 20, on your right.

Voyageuse:	Le prochain train pour Paris part à quelle heure, Monsieur?	What time does the next train for Paris leave, Sir?
Employé:	À midi, Madame. Voilà l'horaire.	At noon, Ma'am. Here's the schedule.
Voyageuse:	Bon, alors je voudrais un aller-retour en seconde.	Good, then I'd like a round-trip ticket in second class.
Employé:	Voilà le billet. Ça fait 200,00 francs.	Here's the ticket. It's 200 francs.

M. Diouf:	Madame...pour aller à l'Hôtel Couronne?	Ma'am...how do I get to the Couronne Hotel?
Mme Poulain:	Prenez l'autobus numéro 2 et descendez à la poste. L'hôtel est à gauche.	Take bus number 2 and get off at the post office. The hotel is on the left.

Exercises

A Match the English with the French.

1. Attendez.   _____   a)   a round-trip ticket

2. je voudrais   _____   b)   on the right

3. à gauche   _____   c)   Where do we board?

4. Descendez à la poste. _____   d)   Here's the schedule.

5. On monte où?   _____   e)   Get off at the post office.

6. Prenez l'autobus.   _____   f)   You must have it.

7. un aller-retour   _____   g)   Wait.

8. Il faut l'avoir.   _____   h)   I would like

9. Voilà l'horaire.   _____   i)   Take the bus.

10. à droite   _____   j)   on the left

B Comment voyages-tu? Complète chaque phrase en français.

1. Je voyage _____ .

2. Je voyage _____ .

3. Je voyage _____ .

4. Je voyage _____ .

5. Je voyage _____ .

C Réponds aux questions.

1. Where do you go to take a train?
   - a) à l'aéroport
   - b) au contrôle des passeports
   - c) à la gare
   - d) dans la rue

2. What do you ask if you want directions to the train station?
   - a) Et on monte où?
   - b) Pour aller à la gare?
   - c) Le train part à quelle heure?
   - d) Est-ce que je peux vous aider?

3. What would you look at to find the times when trains, buses, planes, etc. arrive and leave?
   - a) l'horaire
   - b) le guichet
   - c) le passeport
   - d) la valise

4. What would you say if you wanted to buy a ticket?
   - a) Voilà mon passeport.
   - b) Je voudrais un billet.
   - c) Où vas-tu?
   - d) Pour aller à la poste?

5. If you don't want a first-class ticket, what do you say?
   - a) un aller-retour
   - b) un billet
   - c) l'autobus numéro 2
   - d) en seconde

D Écris les mots correctement.

1. cutigeh _____

2. rohiear _____

3. levisa _____

4. yogrueva _____

5. soperapts _____

E Lis le passage. Choisis les réponses applicables.

Il fait beau aujourd'hui. Fabienne et Éric vont voyager en train. Ils sont au guichet de la gare où Fabienne achète deux billets pour Bordeaux. Les grands-parents de Fabienne habitent près de[1] Bordeaux. Les deux amis compostent[2] leurs billets. Ils attendent le train sur le quai[3] numéro 4. Le train arrive dans la gare à quatorze heures. Quand il arrive, ils montent dans le train. Fabienne choisit une place près de la fenêtre. Les amis parlent de leur visite à Bordeaux où il y a beaucoup à faire. Ils sont heureux. En arrivant ils prennent l'autobus à la maison des grands-parents de Fabienne.

1. Où sont Fabienne et Éric?
   a) à l'aéroport   b) dans l'autobus
   c) dans un taxi   d) à la gare

2. Où voyagent Fabienne et Éric aujourd'hui?
   a) à Lille   b) à Bordeaux
   c) à Rouen   d) à Lyon

3. Combien de billets achète Fabienne?
   a) deux   b) un
   c) quatorze   d) quatre

4. Où est le train?
   a) près de la fenêtre   b) au guichet
   c) sur le quai numéro 4 d) dans les valises

5. Comment vont-ils à la maison des grands-parents de Fabienne?
   a) en train   b) en autobus
   c) en voiture   d) en navire

[1]**près de** = near   [2]**compostent** = stamp   [3]**quai** = platform

F Complete the analogies.

1. employé: _____ = voyageur: voyageuse

2. avion: aéroport = train: _____

3. navire: océan = autobus: _____

4. employé: _____ = professeur: bureau

5. une: deux = première: _____

142

Mots croisés

Vertical	Horizontal

Vertical

1. What you pack your clothes in.
2. A female clerk.
3. What you show at passport control.
6. A street.
7. Opposite of "gauche."
8. «...à la poste.»
12. A child.
13. A plane.
14. «Le train...à midi.»
16. «...fait 200,00 francs.»

Horizontal

1. A female traveler.
4. «Pour...à l'Hôtel Couronne?»
5. «Le prochain train...Bordeaux part à midi.»
9. «Et on...où?»
10. Where.
11. «Je voyage...train.»
12. «Mon passeport...dans ma valise.»
13. "Un...-retour."
15. Good.
17. Wait.

TAXIS PARIS

Un compteur intérieur
3 Tarifs : A. B. C.

Un appareil horaire
sur la plage arrière

Un lumineux TAXI et des voyants
indiquant le tarif appliqué

Une affichette sur la vitre
arrière gauche

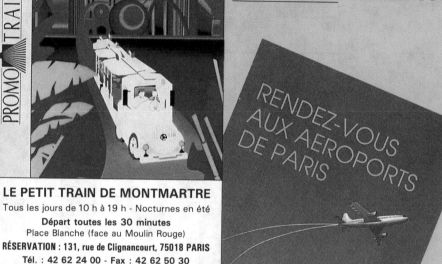

63 **BUS** 63

Porte de la Muette

Gare de Lyon

l'esprit libre

RATP
CARNET 2cl.
SECTION URBAINE

RATP SNCF
COUPON MENSUEL
2 JUIN
ZONES 1 à 2
76867

RATP